BUILDING BETTER

APPLICATIONS

RELATED TITLES FROM VAN NOSTRAND REINHOLD

- Flow-Based Programming: A New Approach for Application Development
  Paul Morrison

- Exploiting Chaos: Cashing in on the Realities of Software Development
  Dave Olson

- Object-Oriented Software Development: Engineering Software for Reuse
  John McGregor and David Sykes

- Data-Modeling Essentials: Analysis Design and Innovation
  Graeme Simsion

- Software Architecture and Design: Principles, Models, and Methods
  Bernard Witt, F. Terry Baker, and Everett Merritt

- Software Testing Techniques
  Boris Beizer

- Testing Computer Software
  Cem Kaner, Jack Falk, and Hung Quoc Nguyen

- Configuration Management for Software
  Steve Compton and Guy Conner

BUILDING BETTER

APPLICATIONS

A THEORY OF EFFICIENT SOFTWARE DEVELOPMENT

Michael R. Dunlavey

VAN NOSTRAND REINHOLD
An International Thomson Publishing Company

New York • London • Bonn • Boston • Detroit • Madrid • Melbourne • Mexico City
Paris • Singapore • Tokyo • Albany NY • Belmont CA • Cincinnati OH

Library of Congress Catalog Card Number 94-4227
ISBN 0-442-01740-5

I(T)P Van Nostrand Reinhold is an International Thomson Publishing company.
       ITP logo is a trademark under license.

Printed in the United States of America

Van Nostrand Reinhold   International Thomson Publishing GmbH
115 Fifth Avenue   Königswinterer Strasse 418
New York, New York 10003   53227 Bonn
                                      Germany

International Thomson Publishing
Berkshire House   International Thomson Publishing Asia
168-173 High Holborn   221 Henderson Road
London WC1V 7AA   #05 10 Henderson Building
                                      Singapore 0315

Thomas Nelson Australia
102 Dodds Street   International Thomson Publishing Japan
South Melbourne, Victoria 3205   Hirakawacho Kyowa Building, 3F
Australia   2-2-1 Hirakawa-cho, Chiyoda-ku
                                      Tokyo 102
Nelson Canada   Japan
1120 Birchmount Road
Scarborough, Ontario
M1K 5G4, Canada

ARCFF 16 15 14 13 12 11 10 9 8 7 6 5 4 3 2 1

Library of Congress Cataloging-in-Publication Data

Dunlavey, Michael R.
    Building better applications : a theory of efficient software
development / Michael R. Dunlavey.
        p.   cm.
    Includes bibliographical references and index.
    ISBN 0-442-01740-5
    1. Computer software—Development.   I. Title.
QA76.76.D47D86   1994
005.1—dc20   94-4227
                                                  CIP

. . . to Mary

and

. . . to the spirit of Thomas Edison.

Contents

Preface

In his provocative article "No Silver Bullet" (*Computer*, April 1987), Fred Brooks painted a fairly bleak future for software development. However, I believe that there are silver bullets, and this volume presents a number of them—examples of programs being made smaller, faster, and more maintainable by large factors.

Herein are demonstrated technical, scientific programming methods for expert programmers, present and future, and their managers and teachers. I am not one to accept the status quo just because thousands of people agree on it. When we ask "Is this the best we can do?" that is a scientific question, and the scientific answer may surprise us.

The content of this volume draws from both academia and the real world. I believe that real-world applications can benefit greatly from theory when the theory is properly chosen and used. I also believe that academia can benefit from exposure to real-world problems, which are always much richer and more interesting than those that may be imagined in the ivory tower.

All programs used in this book are on the accompanying diskette. The examples are nearly all in the C language; some are in C++. Because one of the major thrusts of this approach is to minimize the use of explicit data structure, and because one can think of C++ as C plus data structure classes, few of the examples would look any different in C++, because the examples de-emphasize data.

The theme of this book is that there is hope; that maybe it's not necessary for our future to be dominated by unwieldy, inefficient, million-line behemoth software. To accomplish this is not just a technical problem, but a people problem. If the industry learns that *less is more*, then we have a chance.

The ideas in this book arose through my earlier exposure to programming at Massachusetts Institute of Technology, where the spirit of invention thrives. In particular, the professors and students at the Artificial Intelligence Laboratory were instrumental in the growth of these ideas. I must also thank the many clients I have consulted over the years for giving me great problems to solve. The Boston Chapter of the IEEE Computer Society provided encouragement and a forum for discussion. Students of the seminar I gave, particularly George Rappolt and Mike Ellis, were very helpful in providing feedback and in boosting my confidence. The editors at Van Nostrand Reinhold, Risa Cohen and Christopher Curioli, were very patient and encouraging. Of course, my parents, my dear wife Mary, and our children have for years put up with my great and driving interest in this subject.

Michael R. Dunlavey

Needham, Massachusetts

BUILDING BETTER

APPLICATIONS

1

Speed

Speed, like sex, gets attention. A title I had considered for this book was *Making Software Fast*—a phrase purposely ambiguous, implying that making software faster and making software more quickly are strongly interrelated. If the processes of executing software and of writing it are both considered as having a certain amount of input and output, some useful parallels are presented. To capture this, it is handy to use the vocabulary of *information theory*, in which one asks how efficiently information can be *encoded* in physical data. If there is *noise* (errors), there may be a need for *redundancy* to detect and correct it. The speed of an algorithm or human process becomes its *bandwidth*.

This book is really about the productivity of software developers, but I have found (and I will show) that software is often more complex than necessary and slower than necessary; this due to misplaced concerns about performance. If *speed* is properly understood, it should result in software that both runs faster and is faster to develop.

LOW-LEVEL METHODS

Computers execute software at unbelievable rates, but they still aren't fast enough. Computer makers feverishly vie with one another to bring out each new generation of faster-yet processors. A simple fact, however, is often overlooked: *Execution time depends on both cycle time and the number of instructions executed.* While hardware engineers strive to reduce cycle times, no comparable effort is being spent on

1

the software side. This is a shame because, while exponential hardware speedups come with heroic effort, exponential software slowdowns are thoughtlessly easy to produce.

When analyzing software performance, it is useful to distinguish between the program and the problem. If you consider all of the possible programs that are solutions to the same problem, some one (or a few) of them consumes fewer instruction cycles than the others, so that number of cycles is the best you can do. This number really exists, even if you don't know what it is. When you make a program faster, you are getting closer to it.

There is a useful way to think about problems that helps you to find nearly optimal programs for them; this is to view problems as requiring that a certain amount of information be processed.

Suppose you are a program, and you have a lookup table of eight entries (people's names, for example), and a user is about to ask you to find one of them. Since you don't have any idea which entry she will ask for, you might say you have an uncertainty of eight. Another way to express your uncertainty is through how many conditional branch instructions you have to execute to get to the answer, which is three, right? (If it were one, you could only get to one of two answers, and if it were two, you could only get to one of four answers.) You could say that you have a 3-branch problem. You could also say you have a 3-bit problem, since a conditional instruction you haven't yet executed is like a coin you haven't yet tossed. It takes 1 bit of information to represent its outcome.

Any program is like an information channel that receives a certain number of bits of input information and produces a certain number of bits of output. This is not the same as the amount of *data* that goes in or out. Rather, it has to do with taking the logarithm (base 2) of the number of possibilities. This is shown by the simple diagram in Figure 1.1.

Figure 1.1 demonstrates that the number of information bits (I) in some event is the $\log_2$ of the inverse of its probability ($1/p$). Therefore, if the probability of something is $1/8$, regardless of how many data bits it contains (like someone's name), it has information value of only 3 bits. You can think of this as the amount

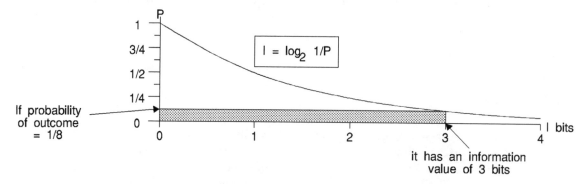

Figure 1.1. The relation between probability of an outcome and its informative value in bits.

of *work* you as a program must do to answer the query. The only question now is how few cycles you can do it in.

A decision point in a program has two or more outcomes, and each outcome has a certain probability and a certain information yield given by the curve in Figure 1.1. If you want to get the most information possible out of taking the branch, you have to adjust the probabilities to maximize the expected (i.e., the average) information yield. This is the information you get from each outcome multiplied by the probability of that outcome, summed over all the outcomes. For example, if your branch point has only two outcomes (Figure 1.2), the information you can expect to get from each outcome is what the outcome would yield times the probability of that outcome. Therefore, if the first outcome yields 1 bit half the time, and the second outcome yields 1 bit half the time, each outcome has an expected yield of ½ bit, and the total expected yield is 1 bit, as you would expect. This measure is called *entropy*, and all it means is the information yield you can expect.

The reason this is important is that you want to get the most information, on the average, out of your decision points, so your work will be done sooner. Unfortunately, when using a decision with only two outcomes, you can't get any more than 1 bit of yield, and that is only if both outcomes are equally likely. Anything that unbalances the outcomes reduces the average information yield (Figure 1.3).

One way to go faster is to use decision points with more than two outcomes. For example, a decision with four equally likely outcomes would have an expected information yield of 2 bits (Figure 1.4), because the sum of the individual yields is 2 bits. An example of a four-outcome decision is a *switch* statement in the C language, or a jump table in assembly language. The more outcomes there are, the greater the expected information yield. For example, a branch having 1024 equiprobable outcomes would yield 10 bits.

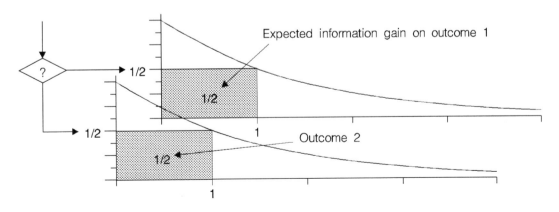

Figure 1.2. The expected information gain (entropy) of a decision is the sum of each outcome's contribution to the average. In the case of a balanced binary decision, the expected information gain is 1 bit.

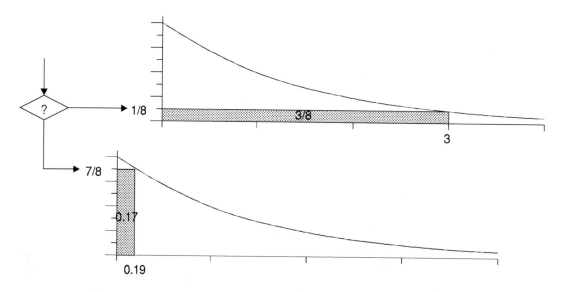

Figure 1.3. Unbalanced decisions yield less information. If the probabilities are ⅛ vs. ⅞, the expected gain is only ⅜ + 0.17 = 0.545 bits, even though one outcome, if it occurs, yields 3 bits.

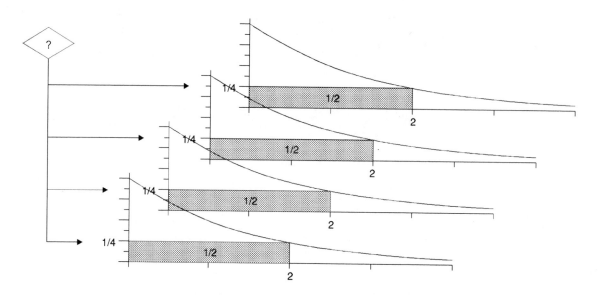

Figure 1.4. To get increased information yield, increase the number of outcomes. A balanced four-way decision point (jump table) yields an average of 2 bits.

The information yield of decisions can help in understanding searching algorithms. Binary search is search using balanced (or nearly balanced) decision points. Indexed search (i.e., direct index to the answer) is search using an N-way decision point, where N is the size of the table. Hash-coded search is search in which the first decision point has many outcomes because it is indexing to a hash bucket, followed by a secondary search within the bucket. On the other hand, linear search is slow because the initial decision points are so unbalanced that they yield very little information.

Binary search is typically presented as using three-way decision points; however, the decision points may as well be two-way since the center outcome is so unlikely that its contribution to the yield is negligible (Figure 1.5).

Information flow can also help in understanding sorting algorithms. Just think of sorting N items as performing N searches, one for each item, to figure out where it belongs in the list.

There are practical points to this theory. It can give you insight into the behavior of basic algorithms. More important, it gives you a deeper insight, causing you to ask what information a program is processing rather than just what data it is processing. Furthermore, it gives a new appreciation for the importance of the machine instructions underlying modern languages. Performance is not a matter of language abstraction; it is a matter of the number of cycles it takes to generate the necessary information yield.

I think it is important to clearly distinguish two areas of concern. Performance is one area, and maintainability is another. These two are not necessarily in

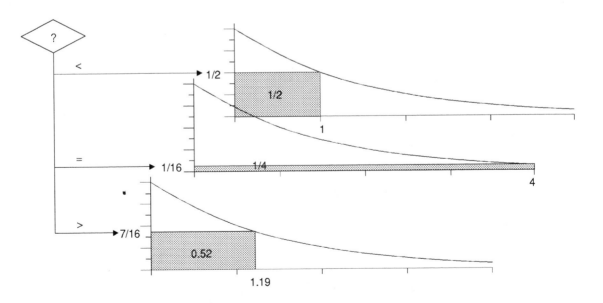

Figure 1.5. Even though binary search uses a three-way decision, it is nearly a two-way balanced decision because the center outcome is so unlikely.

competition for your allegiance, but when they are, you should recognize that there are times when one of them assumes overriding importance. For example, some of the ways we can make programs run fast may seem to make them less maintainable. But there are times when performance is the overriding need. Similarly, there are times when maintainability is the overriding need and performance is less important. Give yourself permission to be aggressive about one, at the expense of the other, when it makes sense.

As an example, you can think of a simple program loop as a linear search for the end point. If the loop is tight, meaning that the time taken by the looping instructions is a significant part of the total time, one can save cycles by *unrolling* the loop, that is, having multiple copies of its body code. A beautiful example of this is the following binary search algorithm. The table to be searched is rounded up to a power of 2, such as 256. If there is not enough data to fill the table, the excess table space is filled with a very large number. The code is:

```
i = 0;
if (key >= table[i +128]) i +=  128;
if (key >= table[i + 64]) i +=   64;
if (key >= table[i + 32]) i +=   32;
if (key >= table[i + 16]) i +=   16;
if (key >= table[i +  8]) i +=    8;
if (key >= table[i +  4]) i +=    4;
if (key >= table[i +  2]) i +=    2;
if (key >= table[i +  1]) i +=    1;
if (key == table[i]) ... then found ...;
```

HIGH-LEVEL METHODS

The above considerations may seem distant from the issue of performance in *large* software, but they are not. They come into play as a kind of end game after larger sources of inefficiency have been removed. The large sources of inefficiency are generally due to unnecessary work being requested, either in the form of needless subroutine calls or needless messages. This extra complexity is often due, ultimately, to misplaced concerns about performance.

The way I get performance in large software is a twofold approach:

1. When designing, I try to keep things as simple as possible, along the lines of the linguistic methodology outlined in Chapter 5. This means identifying what information goes in, goes out, and is stored, and what is the best representation for it, whether as data, program, or both. I specifically avoid anticipation of performance issues, for example, in selecting algorithms. The watchword is *keep it simple*. In particular, this means *the less data structure the better*. It also means being shy of *event-driven* methods.

2. During development and testing, I periodically do performance diagnostics using the methods described below. For synchronous software, the method I use

is random-time sampling of the call stack. For asynchronous software, the method I use is time-line analysis. The nature of this work is that it is not worthwhile trying to guess where the performance problems are. The diagnostics are very good and they tell me exactly where the problems are, so I don't have to waste time on intelligent-sounding, but incorrect, educated guesses. Generally, what actually needs to be fixed is fairly minor.

Sometimes point 1 above (keeping it simple) has not been done, and it is still necessary to tune for performance. That's okay, because point 2 (use diagnostics) still works. Since the software is complicated, however, the diagnostics will find more performance problems, which can be fixed. I have never seen software that was both complex and fast, except software to which diagnostics have already been applied, even if the complexity was intended to solve an anticipated performance problem.

Diagnostic: Call-Stack Sampling

For performance diagnosis, the fundamental information you need to know is, for a given line of code, *how much execution time would be saved if that line were eliminated*. Plenty of popular techniques do not tell you this. For example, counting how many times a line of code or a subroutine is executed does not tell you this. Measuring the elapsed time of subroutines, or anything else, does not tell you this. Compiling statistics of who-calls-who does not tell you this. Sampling the program counter does tell you this, but only for instructions at the bottom of the call stack. What good is there in knowing there are hot spots in system libraries?

One thing, however, *does* tell you what you need to know, and that is the call stack (Figure 1-6). If a line of code is responsible for $x\%$ of total execution time it will be on the call stack $x\%$ of the time (in synchronous software). All you have to do is halt the program at random times, recording the call stack each time. Any line of code that appears on the call stack, say, 50% of the time, more or less, would, if eliminated, save 50% of the total execution time. You don't need thousands of samples to see this. I usually take between 10 and 20 samples, manually, by hitting Control-C in a debugger. Any problem big enough to worry about will show up in that number of samples.

Diagnostic: Time-Line Analysis

Many of today's large systems consist of asynchronous communicating parallel processes, often running on distributed hardware. This makes it hard to tell what a process is really waiting for. Instead of analysis one often hears excuses: "Well, it can't go any faster because it's waiting for the terminal to respond." It is generally impossible to halt a distributed set of machines to examine their collective state. I don't have an easy technique to speed these up, but I do have a difficult one.

Step 1 is to make each individual process as fast as possible when it is not waiting for a message. Usually the pattern is that a process receives a message, does some work (including perhaps sending another message), and goes back to

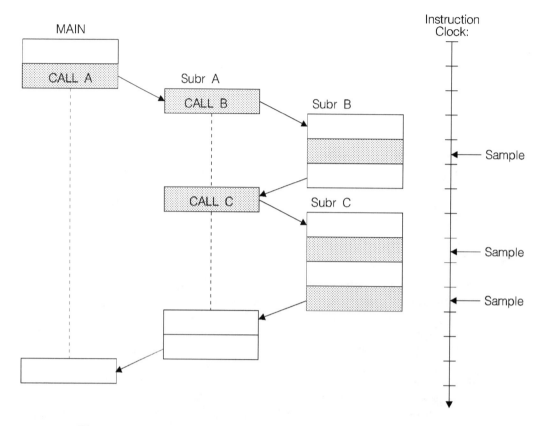

Figure 1.6. Call instructions are responsible for large numbers of cycles being spent. During this time, they are displayed on the call stack. A few random-time samples are sufficient to locate them.

waiting. It is important to optimize this work. The sampling technique can be used for this, if you discard all samples in which the process is waiting for input.

Step 2 is to have a way of collecting, for each process, a time-stamped log of all significant events, such as messages sent, messages received, and message handlers dispatched.

Step 3 is to take the resulting logs and chart them on a long time line (I make my own graph paper). You are looking for delays between the time a message is sent and the time it is received, or between the time it is received and the time it is acted upon; then, you determine why the delay occurred. Often the cause is as simple as a single server handling varying-length transactions, and a short transaction has to wait for a long one to complete. Simply altering priorities, or splitting off a separate process for the slow transactions, may solve the problem. More significant, you may find that needless messages are flowing, and the fact that they are needless is not obvious from the viewpoint of any single process (Figure 1.7).

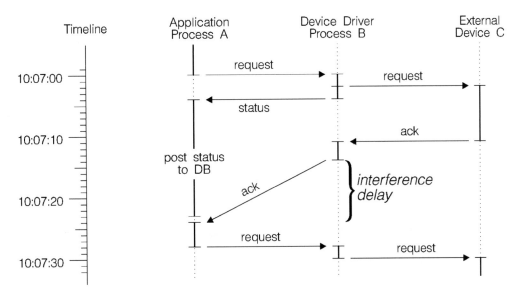

Figure 1.7. Time-line analysis of asynchronous processes can identify artificial delays and extraneous messages.

This method is tedious. It takes me about one full working day to generate a run of event logs, graph them together, and discover things that can be done to speed it up. (No doubt some kind of tool could be built.) Nevertheless, it is often a revelation to find that networks of asynchronous communicating processes can be made to run very fast, even without necessarily using higher communication bit rates.

Example:

Once on a 68000-based UNIX system the following code seemed to be taking longer than it should. This code was a loop involving indexing over an array of structures:

```
struct {
  ....
  }
a[..];

int i;

while(...){
  ..........
  ...a[i]...
  ..........
  }
```

Running this program under the UNIX profiler showed only heavy use of the math library. There didn't seem to be any math called for in the loop. However, we ran it under the debugger and halted it manually (with the hot key, not with a break point). The program counter was inside the library routine for multiplying 32-bit integers. Printing out the call stack showed why. It was being called from the instructions that calculate *a[i]*. To get the address of *a[i]* the index *i* has to be multiplied by the size of the array element. On the 68000 there is no 32-bit multiply instruction, only a 16-bit. Since in that compiler type *int* was 32 bits, the compiler generated a library call. The fix was simply to declare *i* as *short*. The loop tripled in speed.

This example is instructive. The cause of the problem could not easily have been guessed. The profiler only showed *what* the machine was doing, not *why*. Since the program was spending ⅔ of its time in the library routine, the probability was ⅔ that any given sample would find it there, with the guilty CALL instruction waiting on the stack. Removing the CALL instruction eliminated ⅔ of the execution time (except for the multiply instruction that replaced it, which was a lot faster).

Example:

An embedded program on an industrial graphic workstation (ca. 1980) was displaying floating point numbers, and the program seemed to be taking much longer than necessary. Being embedded software, it was not easily instrumented. There was much guesswork as to what could speed up the display, such as adding a math coprocessor, tinkering with the operating system, and so on. However, making the effort to use an in-circuit emulator paid off. When the processor was halted while it was displaying numbers, it turned out to be in the floating-point emulation library. That alone was not a surprise, since floating point numbers were being printed. However, tracing return addresses led back to the following code:

```
float num, newnum;
char digit;

while(...){
    newnum = (int)(num / 10);
    digit = num - newnum * 10 + '0';
    num = newnum;
    ... store digit for output ...
    }
```

What this does is print a floating point number (we had had to write our own *printf*). It peels off digits by doing floating divide, float-to-fix, fix-to-float, floating multiply, floating subtract, and float-to-fix *on every single digit*. Each of these floating-point library operations takes from 100 to 300 instructions. The fix was trivial—converting the number to fixed point and printing it in that form.

Once again, the true problem resisted being guessed. None of the proposed solutions would have really solved it. None of the other common performance analysis techniques would have found it. But a single sampling of the call stack nailed the problem.

I have come to call these things *slugs* (slowness bugs). The process of removing them is called *deslugging* or *slugging it out*.

CASE: CIM SIMULATION

This section gives a state-of-the-art piece of complex simulation software, as an example program to be speeded up. It is a simplified composite of software I have worked on over the years. First we will speed it up by a factor of four. Then we will redesign it and speed it up by an additional factor of ten. The redesigned program will be four times smaller than the first, and it will be easier to modify.

To illustrate this process, I use a program that simulates a computer-integrated manufacturing (CIM) application (Appendix B). The program is a bit large for a sample program, but it is very small for a CIM application. The most interesting slugs appear when a program is large enough to need a few layers of subroutines. First I will present the design of the program. Then I will show how it was deslugged in stages. Then I will show how it was redesigned to be not only much faster, but much smaller and clearer as well!

The Problem

In CIM cell-control applications, there often are four principal functions:

1. *Schedule execution (ISCH in this program)*. This function takes requests for individual manufacturing JOBs. A job consists of a sequence of OPERATIONs. ISCH fits these into a schedule, allocates resources for them, and dispatches them for processing. When all operations of a job are done, it sends completion information back to the requestor.
2. *Task coordination (ITC in this program)*. This function takes requests for operations on jobs and controls their execution. An operation consists of a series of TASKs, such as: command material handling (IMH) to start moving the part to the machining center; command device control (IDEV) to start downloading the tool path file; wait for both tasks to complete; validate the bar code on the part; instruct the machining center to begin cutting; wait for it to finish; upload status information; command material handling to move the part to storage.
3. *Device control (IDEV)*. This function takes requests for machine-related functions, such as tool path download, cycle start and stop, and status monitoring, and it talks to the actual machine to get the machine related function done. In our simulation, this is just a null operation (no-op).

4. *Material handling (IMH).* This function takes care of moving parts from here to there. It talks to the actual controllers. In our simulation, this is just a no-op.

The standard way to design such a system is with a message-flow diagram that contains four big message handlers, each taking in requests and issuing acknowledgments when those requests are satisfied. Each handler in turn sends requests to the handler below it and receives acknowledgments. Each handler keeps a list of outstanding requests and the completion status of each. The handler uses this list to decide what to do next whenever something happens. The design is event-driven. The main entry point is a message dispatch loop, just as in Microsoft Windows. The loop takes each queued message and passes it to the proper function handler. That handler will most likely put more messages in the queue.

In addition to the major function, some utilities are needed. The "cluster" paradigm (related to object-oriented programming [OOP]) is a state-of-the-art way to design these. They are as follows:

1. *List cluster (ILST).* This includes primitives for creating linked lists, deleting them, appending to them, iterating over them, and so on.
2. *Transaction cluster (ITRN).* A transaction is a queued message. There are primitives for creating, deleting, sending, and receiving them.

First Deslugging Pass

The simulation program runs 100 simulated jobs. Each job has ten plus or minus five operations, and each operation has ten tasks—five device and five material handling. As each job completes, the message "Ack Job *nn*" is printed. All in all, the program has to perform 100 jobs, about 1000 operations, and about 10,000 tasks.

The program takes 48 seconds to complete. Granted, it is doing a lot, but think a bit about the timing. If it does 10,000 tasks (each of which is a no-op) in about 50 seconds, it is doing about 200 per second. That is about 1 task every 5 milliseconds, or around 5000 instructions per task, assuming a 1-MIP machine. What is it about a no-op task that takes 5000 instructions to perform? What could be done to speed it up?

The first thing that comes to mind is the transaction queueing mechanism. Shouldn't it be replaced with something handwritten in assembly language? Resisting that temptation, we turn instead to a debugger. I use Microsoft's CodeView. You compile the program using the "-Zi" flag, and then say "CV /I MAIN" to run the program. F5 is the GO key, and Control-C halts the program. Let it run a little bit and then halt it. After you halt it, display the call stack and write it down. You can do this either by typing Alt-C, or by giving the "k" command. If you repeat this several times, a pattern will soon emerge.

You find that the program is spending around 60% of its time in the ILST cluster, in functions ILST_NTH, ILST_NEXT, and ILST_LENGTH. What should you do? You might be tempted to try to fully optimize these routines, especially since they appear to be inefficient, always running down the list from the beginning. Or you might be tempted to scuttle the ILST cluster altogether by going to all 50 or so places the cluster is used and replacing it with something else. Or you might again be tempted to rewrite the transaction cluster, because it is based on the ILST cluster.

Most of the time, however, the ILST routines are being called from routine ITC_PROCESS. The call stacks tell you this. In fact, if you examine the specific lines the ILST routines are being called from, you will see one of those silly slugs, namely the following statement:

```
/* IF ALL TASKS DONE, SEND ITC_ACKOP AND DELETE OP */
if (ptop->current_task >= ILST_LENGTH(ptop->tasklist)){
```

The operation variable *current_task* is the index of the next task to perform. This test is being performed solely to determine if the operation is complete, which it is not 90% of the time.

Right above this line is another slug:

```
/* FOR EACH OPERATION REQUEST */
for (   ptop = ILST_FIRST(oplist);
        ptop != NULL;
        ptop = ILST_NEXT(oplist,ptop)
        ){
```

The cluster operation ILST_NEXT is being called to iterate over the list of operation requests. This is an n-squared operation, since ILST_NEXT searches from the beginning of the list. (With "information hiding," who's to know?) A few lines below, the call stacks point to another slug:

```
ptask = ILST_NTH(ptop->tasklist,ptop->current_task);
```

All this slug is doing is extracting a pointer to the current task from the task list. The occurence of the slugs is all due to the stilted way the list cluster is designed and used.

You might be tempted to think this is a lesson in how not to use list clusters. Wrong! It is a lesson in how to find the slugs that are really there, not the ones you imagine. The slugs in other software will be different, but the process of finding them is the same.

The fix is easy. First of all, get rid of the ILST_NEXT in the iteration. Just step a pointer along in the normal way. Second, rather than keeping a numeric index of the next task in the list, keep a pointer to it. This eliminates the need to call the ILST_NTH and ILST_LENGTH primitives. (When the pointer runs off the end and becomes NULL, there are no more tasks.) The result is that execution time drops to about 20 seconds (speedup factor: 2.4), without hand-optimizing anything!

Second Pass

On the second pass, we do as before: Run the program under the debugger, randomly halting it a few times. This time new slugs appear—ones that were there before, but were masked by the big slugs. Again, time is being spent in the ILST cluster, but this time it is spent in the ILST_APPEND primitive (which runs down the list, tacking new items on the end).

Should we make the list cluster more complex, with a pointer to both ends? Fortunately, the call stacks find a more effective fix. Some of the calls occur when the task list of an operation is being created. The following line causes the tasks to be appended to the list one at a time:

```
ILST_APPEND(ptop->tasklist,ptask);
```

This is an n-squared operation because ILST_APPEND runs the length of the list.

Another significant source of calls to ILST_APPEND is this line in ITRN_PUT in the transaction cluster:

```
ILST_APPEND(trnque,ptrn);
```

Finally, we are seeing time spent in transactions!

The fix I made was twofold. To eliminate the time spent appending tasks when building a task list, I just put them in a temporary array and then built the list all at once. I added a routine *ilst_make* to the ILST cluster that would take an array of pointers and make an equivalent list. In the transaction cluster, I changed it to use a circular array for the queue, rather than a list. The result? Execution time dropped to 17 seconds (speedup factor: 2.8).

Third Pass

The slugs are getting smaller now, and there are more of them. I find time being spent on list operations at the operation/job level, and in transaction dispatching. I make the following changes:

In ITRN, I change the cluster to use pointers into the queue rather than indexes.

In ITC, I change pointers l and ptop to be register variables.

In ISCH, I get rid of the use of the ILST cluster on the operation lists, just as I did earlier on the task lists in ITC.

In ITC, time is being spent in the following loop. It is a linear search of the operation list whenever a task completion is received from IDEV.

```
for (l=oplist; l; l=l->next){
        ptop = l->thing;
        if (ptop->id==ptn->tskid) break;
        }
if (ptop==NULL){
        /* ERROR: INVALID OPERATION ID */
        }
```

I replaced it by the following code:

```
for (l=oplist
        ; l && ((operation_t*)l->thing)->id != ptn->tskid
        ; l=l->next){
        }
if (l==NULL){
        /* ERROR: INVALID OPERATION ID */
        }
ptop = l->thing;
```

This seemed to compile into a faster loop. I did the same thing for the same loop on receipt of a material-handling acknowledgment.

In *main*, transaction dispatching is handled by doing a linear table search. When the transaction code is found in the table, the code knows to which routine to send the transaction. I replaced that loop by unrolling it and hard-coding the search because it is pointless to put things in run-time tables if they never change at run time. Result? Execution time was reduced to 13 seconds (speedup factor: 3.7).

Fixes are becoming less easy to find. The call stack tells me what it's doing, but I've already done what I could to speed it up. It is easy to see that it is spending much of its time dispatching transactions and finding relevant operations when acknowledgements are received.

The Redesign

Let's go back to the original problem. It says we have JOBs, each job has OPERATIONs, and each operation has TASKs. If we say this in structured pseudocode, it looks like this:

```
To perform a JOB:
        For each operation of the job
        begin
                Perform the operation
        end

To perform an OPERATION:
        For each task of the operation
        begin
                Perform the device task.
                Perform material handling task.
        end

To perform a device TASK:
        (Simulate a delay.)

To perform a material handling TASK:
        (Simulate a delay.)
```

If the above statement were executable, we would have an implementation. Nowhere does the problem say that we have to have functional modules, transactions, events, and all that. What we really have to do is implement the language that makes this statement run. On the other hand, the basic time sequence of activities has to be pretty much the same as before, if we want to keep the same functionality. To do this, I created a "little language" using some C macros.

What kind of language is it? Since jobs run in parallel with each other, the language must support parallel execution. We don't want to go all the way to a separate process for each job, however. We want to keep things simple, small, and efficient. We want each job to be a lightweight process. Why not use OS/2 or Modula II or Ada? Well, personally I like C, and OS/2 didn't happen to be an option. Besides, even lightweight processes are pretty heavy, what with pre-emptive scheduling, context-switching, and all. I really don't want the final program to behave much differently from the way it does now. I just want to make it cleaner.

The result is contained in Appendix C. The way the language works is that there are processes. A process consists of an application data record, such as a job record, an operation record, or a task record. In the record is a pointer to a control procedure and an integer state variable.

When a new job process is begun, its record is allocated and initialized. Then it is resumed. Resuming consists of calling the record's control procedure. The control procedure does whatever it needs to do and returns, but first it sets the state variable. The next time it is resumed, it dispatches on the state variable and does whatever comes next, and so on. No surprise—it's just a finite state machine.

So, when we start a job, we are just creating a finite state machine. When the job starts an operation, that too is a finite state machine. We can think of it as a subroutine of the job, since the job will wait for the operation to finish before it starts the next operation. In fact, when we create the operation state machine record, we include a pointer to the job's state machine record. This way, when the operation is done, it simply deletes itself and resumes the job.

What does this buy us? It eliminates: (1) the transaction to start an operation, (2) the transaction when an operation completes, and (3) having to do a search to find the job that requested the operation. The same thing is true of the relationship between operations and tasks. So what transactions remain? Only those connected to simulated outside events—device and material handling delays.

Finally, what are the primitives of the language?

```
PROLOGUE(type,f)
```

In this statement *type* is the typedef'ed name of the application record, and *f* is the name of the control procedure. This statement is called from within the process-creation procedure; it expands into all the necessary setup code and resumes the process.

```
DISPATCHn
```

This is the first statement inside the control procedure of a process. In this statement *n* is the number of states in the process; it takes care of dispatching on the state variable whenever the process is resumed.

```
BREAK(n)
```

In this statement *n* is a unique state number. This statement is the non-preemptive release of control to a global process queue; it puts the process in a global queue and gives up control. Later, when the global dispatcher resumes it, the DISPATCH statement sends control to the statement following the BREAK.

You can put BREAK statements anywhere, such as deep inside loops or conditional statements. For example, if you want to busy-wait for some condition to be true, you could say:

```
while (... condition is FALSE ...){
        printf("I'm still waiting\n");
        BREAK(3);
        }
```

BREAK(3) expands into:

```
p->state = 3;
enque(p);
return;
L3:;
```

and DISPATCHn expands into:

```
if (p->state==1) goto L1;
if (p->state==2) goto L2;
if (p->state==3) goto L3;
... up to n ...
```

These macros are generating *goto* statements, so one might wonder: Is this language structured? I claim it is because the goto's are invisible in the source, just as the jump instruction generated by a compiler from if statements are also invisible.

Suppose you realize you need to have the state machine wait for one more thing. Just insert a BREAK statement at the right spot and renumber the states. That is a very easy change to make, which is why I claim this new language made of macros is a problem-oriented language.

```
CALL(n,expr)
```

In this statement *n* is a unique state number, and *expr* creates another process (passing itself as the first argument). This statement does the lightweight-process equivalent of a subroutine call. It creates and resumes a subordinate process. When that process completes, it deletes itself and resumes the current process. The subordinate can return a value.

```
RETURN(v)
```

This is the primitive that effects a lightweight-process return, resuming the calling process and passing it the value v. The RETURN statement knows who the caller is because that was the first argument of the process.

So where does this leave us? The application is one-fourth the size of the first version, even including the definition of the little language. It now gets the job done in ten seconds (speedup factor: 4.8).

Fourth Pass

Now it has hot spots in the *enque* and *deque* routines. I replace these by in-line macros, and the time goes down to seven seconds (speedup factor: 6.9).

Fifth Pass

Most of the time is being spent in printing out the hundred "Ack Job *nn*" messages. Commenting out the printf brings the time down to four seconds (speedup factor: 12).

Sixth Pass

I increase the number of jobs to 1000, to make the program run long enough to observe. I see that it is spending a large percentage of time in *_malloc()* and *_free* as objects are being created and destroyed. So, I recycle used objects in special stacks. Also, in each process, I make the self pointer *p* a register variable. Resulting time is 26 seconds, or 2.6 seconds for 100 jobs (speedup factor: 18.5).

Final Rewrite

Now, the bulk of the time is spent in the CALL and RETURN statements. Since operations and tasks are serialized within each job, there is no need to make them separate processes, so I recode again, according to this pseudocode:

To perform a JOB:

```
For each OPERATION of the job
begin
        For each TASK of the operation
        begin
                (Simulate device task delay.)
                (Simulate material handling task delay.)
        end
end
```

This gets rid of the CALL statements. The result? Eleven seconds, or 1.1 seconds per 100 jobs (speedup factor: 43.6).

The original program took 48 seconds. That consisted of:

28 seconds:	ITC use of list processing
3 seconds:	Transaction queue list processing
	Building lists

4 seconds:	More random list processing and searching
3 seconds:	Request and acknowledgement of transactions
	ID searching on acknowledgements
3 seconds:	Enqueue and dequeue subroutines
3 seconds:	Printing messages to screen
1.4 seconds:	*_malloc()* and *_free()*
1.5 seconds:	Process CALL and RETURN statements
1.1 seconds:	Final time

There you have it.

It is tempting to think that a price in maintainability has been paid for this performance, but suppositions are often wrong. Suppose you are told to add another layer of ten subtasks in place of the single device task, and you have ten minutes to do it. Under the original design, it would be whole design change. Under the final design, it's a three-line edit (add a counter variable to the job record and wrap a loop around the first BREAK statement). What is maintainance about, if it isn't about being able to respond easily to requests?

CONCLUSION

This case study is lengthy, but it illustrates a number of important points which are discussed below.

It shows what performance-tuning is really like—guesswork has no place in the process; the diagnostics are everything. It is an iterative process, each speedup identifying new opportunities for speedup. The first few iterations consisted of removing things that were there for pseudo-religious reasons, such as the desire to use clusters (on the theory that they make maintenance easier). I've got a term for this: *galloping generality*. In my experience, the bigger the software system, the more layers of needlessly general utilities are sapping performance.

After the original program is tuned as far as possible, you have a much better understanding of what it is doing. It may be possible to use this insight to redesign it using a little language. This usually results in better maintainability as well as better performance.

It is important to note that the redesigned program has *less explicit data structure*. This means that to make a change to it there is less "plumbing" to do in the form of adding structures, adding fields to structures, and adding code to store, transfer, and use data in the added fields. The essential data is still there, but it is in the form of state machine records, so the data is more like normal program variables. The nonessential data is not there, such as separate lists of jobs, operations, and tasks. There is no list searching involved in the normal course of operation. I believe this *data minimal programming* will be an important trend in future software.

In redesigning the program, a mental shift occurred. In the original design, the primary concerns were the data objects and activities, in other words, a *run time* perspective. In the redesigned program, the primary concern is the structure of the source code, a *development time* perspective. In the redesign, the problem is not so much *solved* as it is *stated*. The code is closer to being declarative.

What about object-oriented programming (OOP)? You can see that both programs are object-oriented. The first program uses clusters (which are like classes) to represent both application objects and general data structure objects. The second program uses state machines, which are data records paired with a procedure, which is just what an object is. This indicates that OOP by itself has little to do with whether a program is big or small, fast or slow. If the processing involves a flexible number of entities living their lives in parallel, then there has to be OOP going on, at some level of description. Is the second program smaller because it is more effectively reusing code? Hardly. In fact, the first program is large because it is excessively reusing code. The first program uses clusters to simplify the programming of lists and transactions that don't even exist in the second program.

Finally, I stated that much of the slowness of software is due to complexity that arises from concern about performance. In the first design, the whole event-driven architecture with event queues and handlers is, I believe, founded on a fear of polling methods. In the second design, state machines are quite capable of polling for the conditions that allow them to proceed. One of the trickiest things to program in an event-driven architecture is a simple polling loop.

2

Redundancy

Sometime around 1979 I was working for a client who performed all work in assembly language for mini-computers. Often it was necessary for more than one person to work on the same program. This led to considerable headaches, as each person did not know what the other had done to the code. One day, I thought, "Why not have a program to compare Jim's version of the code with mine? When it finds a mismatch, I'll have it scan ahead in both files until it finds matching lines. Then I'll print out the lines that didn't match and keep going" (Figure 2.1). One afternoon I got in the mood, wrote the program, and started using it. Suddenly the angst associated with the need to coordinate programmers disappeared. Each could see, plain as day, what the other had done, and we could easily merge our changes. I didn't know it, but the same problem had already been solved in the UNIX community, in the form of the *diff* utility, and used as the foundation for a powerful source code librarian called *sccs*.

File-differencing utilities such as *diff* address one example of a very fundamental problem, namely *redundancy*. As soon as you have two or more copies of anything, you have to deal with the possibility that the copies might not *agree* with each other. Or, to put it another way, the imaginary collection consisting of both copies together could be inconsistent with itself. There are many kinds of redundancy, and redundancy is a matter of degree. Redundancy may often be beneficial or simply necessary, but it always has a price, and the greater the redundancy, the greater the price.

There are two complementary attitudes to take toward redundancy. First, *avoid it* (aggressively if need be). Second, *when you cannot avoid it, deal with it squarely*. The case of maintaining source code is a good example. There shouldn't be lots of

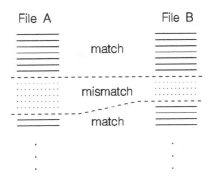

Figure 2.1. To compare two files, the mismatching lines must be found.

slightly different copies of source files floating around. However, people have a common mission and they do need to work, and they often need to work on the same files at the same time. It's just a fact. So, they need a tool such as *diff* that enables them to reconcile differences, which is squarely facing the redundancy problem.

I present a simple *diff* algorithm here, because it is instructive to see a way of modeling this process and because you can adapt it to other problems.

The diagram in Figure 2.2 illustrates matching two files. If two lines, such as line 0 in file A and line 0 in file B (<0,0>) are equal, we draw a diagonal line from <0,0> to <1,1>. Then we go to that new pair of lines and repeat. When we get to <2,2> the lines are not equal, so we initiate a search pattern. To search forward from the point <i,j> we try:

$$<i+1, j>, <i, j+1>$$
$$<i+2, j>, <i+1, j+1>, <i, j+2>$$
$$<i+3, j>, <i+2, j+1>, <i+1, j+2>, <i, j+3>$$

and so on until we find an equal pair of lines. If we sync up at <i+m, j+n>, then we have a mismatch of m lines from file A and n lines from file B.

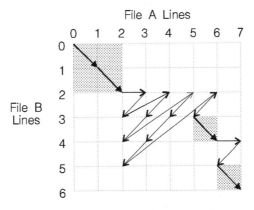

Figure 2.2. Comparing files. When a mismatch is encountered, a search pattern finds the next pair of matching lines.

This algorithm is not the most efficient because it is quadratic in the size of the differences. A better version would index the lines of file 2 in some sort of hash table so that the search could be done more quickly.

Another problem with this algorithm is that it matches too easily. For example, it considers two blank lines as matching even if one is in the middle of a large section of inserted lines. It is possible to refine the algorithm by first searching for matches of more than one line before searching for one-line matches. The programming motif of having two (or more) structures and resolving differences by means of a coordinated iteration pattern is nevertheless a very useful tool for dealing with redundancy. (The classic sorted merge algorithm is probably the most familiar example.)

A SIMPLE FILE-DIFFERENCING PROGRAM

A simple file-differencing program is given here. It can be used as is or adapted to different purposes.

```
1  /* MDIFF.C  FILE DIFFERENCER */
2
3  #include <stdio.h>
4
5  /* STRUCTURES A AND B CONTAIN LINES FROM FIRST FILE AND SECOND FILE */
6  struct buf_struct {
7      int nline;      /* NUMBER OF LINES */
8      char *buf;      /* FILE BUFFER */
9      char **line;    /* POINTERS TO LINES */
10     };
11
12 struct buf_struct a, b;     /* THE TWO FILE STRUCTURES */
13
14 /* READFILE: READ FILE AND FILL BUFFER STRUCTURE.  IF FAILURE, RETURN 0 */
15 int readFile(char *fname, struct buf_struct *p){
16     FILE * f=NULL;
17     int i=0,n=0,i1=0,c=0;
18     /* OPEN THE FILE */
19     f = fopen(fname,"r");
20     if (f==NULL) return 0;
21     /* COUNT THE NUMBER OF LINES AND CHARACTERS */
22     p->nline = 1;
23     while((c=getc(f)) != EOF){
24             n++;
25             if (c=='\n') p->nline++;
26             }
27     /* GET READY TO READ AGAIN */
28     fseek(f, 0L, SEEK_SET);
29     /* ALLOCATE BUFFER SPACE AND ARRAY OF LINES */
30     p->buf = (char*)malloc(n + 10);
31     if (p->buf==NULL) return 0;
32     memset(p->buf, 0, n + 10);
33     p->line = (char**)malloc(sizeof(char*)*(p->nline+1));
34     if (p->line==NULL) return 0;
35     memset(p->line, 0, sizeof(char*)*(p->nline+1));
36     /* READ THE LINES INTO THE BUFFER */
```

```
37      i1 = i = 0;
38      p->line[i1++] = p->buf + i;
39      while((c=getc(f)) != EOF){
40              p->buf[i++] = c;
41              if (p->buf[i-1]=='\n'){
42                      p->buf[i-1] = 0;
43                      p->line[i1++] = p->buf + i;
44                      }
45              }
46      /* NULL TERMINATE BUFFER, AND CLOSE FILE */
47      p->buf[i] = 0;
48      fclose(f);
49      return 1;
50      }
51
52 /* MATCH(IA, IB): TELL IF THE TWO LINES MATCH */
53 int match(int ia, int ib){
54      return strcmp(a.line[ia], b.line[ib])==0 ;
55      }
56
57 /* NREM1 AND NREM2 ARE THE NUMBER OF LINES REMAINING
58      IN EACH FILE */
59 #define NREM1 (a.nline - ia)
60 #define NREM2 (b.nline - ib)
61
62 /* SKIPTOMATCH: DETERMINE SIZE OF MISMATCH STARTING AT IA, IB */
63 void skipToMatch(int ia, int ib, int *pda, int *pdb){
64      int delta, da, db;
65      for (delta = 0; delta <= (NREM1 + NREM2); delta++){
66              for (da = delta, db = 0; da >= 0 ; da--, db++){
67                      if (da==NREM1 && db==NREM2)
68                              goto MATCHED;
69                      else if (da < NREM1 && db < NREM2
70                              && match(ia+da, ib+db)
71                              ) goto MATCHED;
72                      }
73              }
74      MATCHED:;
75      *pda = da;
76      *pdb = db;
77      }
78
79 void main(int argc, char *argv[]){
80      int i, ia, ib;
81      int ndiff = 0;
82
83      if (argc!=3){
84              fprintf(stderr,"Usage: mdiff file-1 file-2\n");
85              exit(1);
86              }
87
88      /* READ IN THE TWO FILES */
89      if (!readFile(argv[1], &a)){
90              fprintf(stderr,"Unable to read file %s\n",argv[1]);
91              return;
92              }
93
94      if (!readFile(argv[2], &b)){
```

```
95              fprintf(stderr,"Unable to read file %s\n",argv[2]);
96              return;
97              }
98
99      /* MAIN MATCHING LOOP */
100     /* the idea is that we skip ia, ib forward from match to match
101             until ia==a.nline and ib==b.nline */
102     /* at each step, we detect and skip over any mismatch in the
103             form of da lines from file a, and db lines from file b
104             where da >= 0 and db >= 0 */
105     ia = 0;
106     ib = 0;
107     while(1){
108             int da, db;
109             /* FIND THE MISMATCH, IF ANY */
110             skipToMatch(ia, ib, &da, &db);
111             /* IF THERE IS A MISMATCH, COUNT IT */
112             if (da > 0 || db > 0) ndiff++;
113             /* PRINT LINES FROM FILE A, IF ANY */
114             for (i = ia; i < ia + da; i++){
115                     printf("-%s\n", a.line[i]);
116                     }
117             /* PRINT LINES FROM FILE B, IF ANY */
118             for (i = ib; i < ib + db; i++){
119                     printf("+%s\n", b.line[i]);
120                     }
121             /* ADVANCE OVER THE MISMATCH */
122             ia += da;
123             ib += db;
124             /* IF AT END OF FILE(S) QUIT */
125             if (ia >= a.nline)
126                     break;
127             /* PRINT MATCHING LINE */
128             printf("%s\n", a.line[ia]);
129             /* ADVANCE OVER IT */
130             ia++;
131             ib++;
132             }
133     fprintf(stderr, "%3d differences\n", ndiff);
134     }
```

Lines 5–50 declare a structure *buf_struct*, and function *readFile* to read a file into a buffer and break it into lines. The method is to read the file twice, once to see how many characters and lines it contains so as to allocate the buffer, and once to read it in.

Lines 52–55 define a Boolean function *match* that tells if two lines are considered to match. All it does is a string compare, but in more sophisticated versions of the algorithm it could do considerably more.

Lines 62–77 are the key function *skipToMatch*. Given that *ia* and *ib* point to the beginnings of a region that may or may not be a mismatch, it returns *da*, the delta size of the mismatch in file A, and *db*, the delta size in file B. It works by scanning ahead in a search pattern until it encounters either a matching line or the end of both files. It is careful not to search beyond the end of either file.

Line 79 begins the main program. First it opens and reads in the two files. Then it enters the main matching loop. It is based on the idea that the files are identical except for the possible mismatch that can occur in front of each pair of matching lines (or the end). Thus, on each iteration it checks for the existence of a mismatch, and if there is one it prints it out. Then it prints the matching lines unless we are at the end.

This version of the program, since it prints all lines, creates a merge of the two files. If a line is in file A but not in file B, it is printed with a hyphen (-) in column 1. Symmetrically, if a line is in file B but not in file A, it is printed with a leading plus sign (+). You can think of this as meaning file A can be changed into file B by removing the (-) lines and adding the (+) lines.

If you wish to print out only the mismatches without the common lines, it is only necessary to comment out line 128. You might then want to print the line numbers of the mismatches, which are available in variables *ia* and *ib*.

Here are two corrupted versions of a text file:

```
poem1.txt:
 1 My heart leaps up when I behold
 2   A rainbow in the sky;
 3 So was it when my life began;
 4 So is is now I am a man;
 5 So be it when I shall grow old.
 6 And I could wish my days to be
 7 Bound each to each by natural piety.
```

```
poem2.txt:
 1 My heart leaps up when I behold
 2   A rainbow in the sky;
 3 So it is now I am a man;
 4 So be it when I shall grow old.
 5   Or let me die!
 6 The Child is father of the man;
 7 And I could wish my days to be
 8 Bound each to by natural piety.
 9   -Wordsworth
```

The program is run by entering *mdiff poem1.txt poem2.txt > poem3.txt* with the following result:

```
poem3.txt
  1  My heart leaps up when I behold
  2    A rainbow in the sky;
  3- So was it when my life began;
  4- So is is now I am a man;
  5+ So it is now I am a man;
  6  So be it when I shall grow old.
  7+   Or let me die!
  8+ The Child is father of the Man;
  9  And I could wish my days to be
 10  Bound each to by natural piety.
 11    —Wordsworth
```

The point of the exercise is that dealing with redundancy can be done with quite simple tools. In this case it is the redundancy of having multiple files that disagree. It permits the mismatches to be resolved, which deals squarely with the redundancy.

DIFFERENTIAL EXECUTION

Another type of unavoidable redundancy has to do with user interface displays. When a program draws or prints a view of some data on a user interface screen, that presentation persists until the screen is erased or otherwise altered. Therefore, the screen has memory, and that memory is redundant with the underlying data from which it was derived. When the underlying data changes, as it does in real-time systems, there is a need to incrementally update the display screen to maintain consistency.

Having faced this situation many times in my professional work, a scheme occurred to me that appears to be a general solution. Differential execution (*difex* for short) is a scheme for running any procedure in such a way that you can always know how the current execution differs from a prior execution. If the procedure is a subroutine to paint a graphic display, you can detect differences from the previous execution, and use these differences to incrementally update the display. In other words, you only have to write a *paint* routine, which is a lot simpler than writing an *incremental-repaint* routine. The paint routine is preferable because, although there is redundancy (unavoidably), there is also an effective way to manage the redundancy so as to reduce programmer errors.

Suppose you have to produce a graphical display of some complex application data and keep the display up-to-date as the data changes in real time. Now suppose the display terminal is at the other end of a slow communications line, so you have to do the updates incrementally. At the same time, you can't update the display after *every* change to the underlying data—it may change tens of times per second. Further suppose you have many displays like this to program in a limited time, and the penalty for showing incorrect information is high.

This type of problem is fairly common in industrial software. The *difex* technique is as follows: Write a routine to paint the desired display as a static image. This routine is called a *display procedure* or *view procedure*, because it produces a static display or view of the data. Even though the display procedure describes a static display, it is used to produce a dynamic display by invoking it repeatedly, say, once per second. Within each display primitive to draw a line segment or text string, decisions are made as to whether that line segment or text string matches what was drawn previously. If it matches, nothing need be sent to the remote display terminal. If not, the object is erased and redrawn or otherwise incrementally updated. To do this, there needs to be a low-level memory of what has been displayed, and this is provided in the form of a "first-in-first-out" memory (FIFO) acting as a sequential delay-line storage. This technique is diagrammed in Figure 2.3.

The technique relies on the repeatability of the sequence of low-level calls, which can be broken if the display procedure contains conditional statements such as IF, FOR, WHILE, SWITCH, etc.

There is, however, a mechanism that can account for conditional statements in a completely general way. It involves recording in the FIFO the value of each conditional expression, so as to detect changes in execution path. The technique has broader utility than just dynamic graphics. For example, it has been used to detect real-time changes in a data base.

To get started, here is some code to declare a FIFO:

```
/* declare the FIFO */
#define QUESIZE 8192
#define QUEPAD 512
char queue[QUESIZE];
char * enq = queue;
char * deq = queue;
```

The FIFO is a linear array. There are two pointers into it, one for putting data in (*enq*), and one for getting data out (*deq*). There are many ways to code a FIFO; this method is optimized for speed. Pointers are faster than using integer indexes. The purpose of the 512-byte pad at the end is to detect wraparound efficiently.

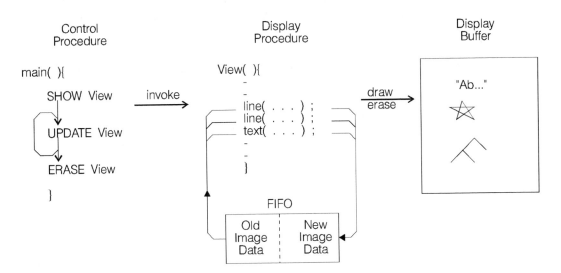

Figure 2.3. Maintaining a dynamic display by using differential evaluation. The control procedure, left, repeatedly invokes a display procedure, center, to maintain a dynamic image in the display buffer, right. Efficiency is achieved by performing incremental redrawing at the level of primitive lines or text strings. This requires memory of what is on the screen, provided in the form of a FIFO acting as a sequential delay line.

When putting or getting data, we don't check for wraparound on every single byte, but only after transferring a whole unit of data such as an integer or character string.

The basic idea is that there is a global mode variable having three values, *SHOW*, *UPDATE*, and *ERASE*.

```
/* declare the mode variable */
int mode;
#define ERASE 1
#define SHOW 2
#define UPDATE (ERASE | SHOW)
```

The mode is set initially to SHOW and the display procedure is invoked. This causes each graphical primitive to generate output to the screen, with the result that the image is painted. Simultaneously with drawing, each primitive is writing its arguments into the FIFO, so that at the end the FIFO contains the end points, text strings, and other arguments of the graphical primitives, packed together in sequential order.

To update the display, the mode is set to UPDATE, and the display procedure is invoked again. In this mode, each graphical primitive also writes its arguments to the FIFO, but it reads its prior arguments (written during the prior invocation) out of the FIFO as well. If the arguments match, no pixels need be drawn. If not, the arguments provide enough information to erase and redraw the primitive.

The technique is completely symmetrical. Just as it can show, it can also erase. If the mode is set to ERASE and the display procedure invoked, each primitive reads its prior arguments out of the FIFO and uses them to erase from the screen what it had drawn there in a prior invocation (Figure 2.4). (This is overkill if all we want to do is to clear the screen, but the ERASE capability turns out to be just what we need to handle conditionals.)

Here is some low-level code to implement this logic. First we will need a couple of routines to put data in and get data from the FIFO:

```
/* put a new text string in the FIFO, and
   get an old one out, depending on the mode */

putgetStr(char * newstr, char * oldstr){
        if (mode != ERASE){
                while (*enq++ = *newstr++);
                if (enq >= queue+QUESIZE-QUEPAD)
                        enq = queue;
                }
        if (mode != SHOW){
                while (*oldstr++ = *deq++);
                if (deq >= queue+QUESIZE-QUEPAD)
                        deq = queue;
                }
```

```
        }
/* put an integer in the FIFO, and get
   an old one out, depending on the mode */

putgetInt(char * newint, char * oldint){
        /* assuming sizeof(int) == 2 */
        if (mode != ERASE){
                *enq++ = *newint++;
                *enq++ = *newint++;
                if (enq >= queue+QUESIZE-QUEPAD)
                        enq = queue;
        }
        if (mode != SHOW){
                *oldint++ = *deq++;
                *oldint++ = *deq++;
                if (deq >= queue+QUESIZE-QUEPAD)
                        deq = queue;
        }
}
```

These routines are used to simplify the coding of display primitives. They ensure that putting and getting of data is done properly in accordance with the mode.

A primitive to maintain a line segment is typical of graphical primitives:

```
/* maintain a line segment on the display */

line(x0, y0, x1, y1)
        int x0; int y0; int x1; int y1;
{
        int oldx0, oldy0, oldx1, oldy1;
        int doerase = mode & ERASE;
        int doshow = mode & SHOW;
        putgetInt(&x0, &oldx0);
        putgetInt(&y0, &oldy0);
        putgetInt(&x1, &oldx1);
        putgetInt(&y1, &oldy1);
        if (mode == UPDATE){
                if (x0==oldx0 && y0==oldy0
                        && x1==oldx1 && y1==oldy1)
                                doshow = doerase = 0;
        }
        if (doerase)
                erase_line(oldx0, oldy0, oldx1, oldy1);
        if (doshow)
                draw_line(x0, y0, x1, y1);
}
```

The arguments to the routine are the new end points of the line segment. (I have used the old style of declaring arguments [non-ANSI] because when we call the primitive in ERASE mode we will have to pass *no* arguments, and we don't want to have to fight with the compiler.) Inside the routine we declare a set of duplicate arguments whose names start with *old*, which will receive the prior argument

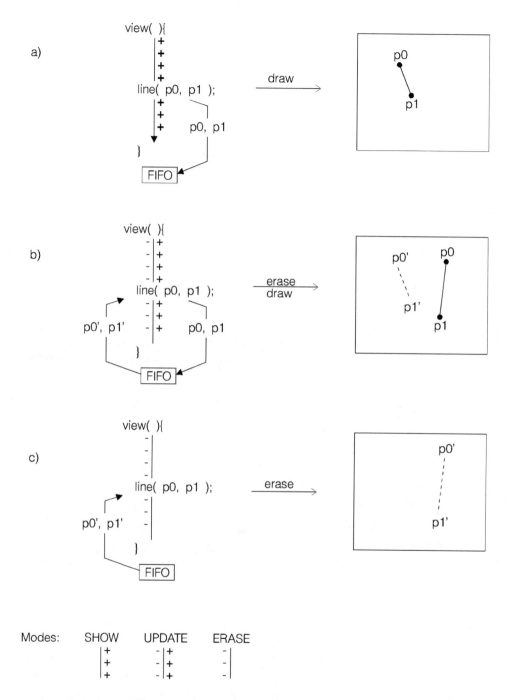

Figure 2.4. Maintenance of a graphical line segment. In SHOW mode (a) the line is drawn and its end points are written to the FIFO. In UPDATE mode (b) the new end points are written, and the prior end points are read from the FIFO. If the end points are different, the line segment is erased and redrawn. In ERASE mode (c) the prior end points are read and the line segment is erased.

values from the FIFO. There are two Boolean variables, *doerase* and *doshow*, that determine if erasing or showing will be done. Notice that we use the bitwise encoding of the mode to save a few cycles here. The first real activity in the routine is to call *putgetInt* to handle the putting of each argument and the getting of its old value. Next we determine how to update the line segment. If the mode is UPDATE we have both old and new values. If the old and new values are equal we should neither erase nor draw the line segment, so we set the two Booleans to zero. Finally, if we need to erase the line segment, we do so using the old values of the arguments (because they represent the current appearance of the line segment). If we need to draw the line segment, we do so using the new arguments.

A graphical version of *printf* works the same way:

```
/* maintain a character string on the display */


text(x,y,fmt,a0,a1,a2,a3,a4,a5)
        int x, y;
        char * fmt;
        int a0, a1, a2, a3, a4, a5;
{
        int oldx, oldy;
        int doerase = mode & ERASE;
        int doshow = mode & SHOW;
        char buf[100], oldbuf[100];
        if (mode & SHOW)
                sprintf(buf,fmt,a0,a1,a2,a3,a4,a5);
        putgetInt(&x, &oldx);
        putgetInt(&y, &oldy);
        putgetStr(buf, oldbuf);
        if (mode == UPDATE){
                if (x==oldx && y==oldy
                        && strcmp(buf, oldbuf)==0)
                                doshow = doerase = 0;
        }
        if (doerase)
                erase_text(oldx, oldy, oldbuf);
        if (doshow)
                draw_text(x, y, buf);
}
```

You may be wondering how we can erase things without damaging overlapping objects. That is really a separate problem from the problem of detecting changes, and I will deal with it separately when the two-phase update is discussed later in this section.

To handle conditionals, the best example is the lowly IF statement. It contains a body of source code and a Boolean test expression. Its meaning is that the graphics described by the body of the statement are to be visible if and only if the test expression has the value TRUE. When the IF statement is executed in SHOW mode it behaves like a normal IF statement except that it also writes the Boolean value of its test expression to the FIFO. Later, when it is executed in UPDATE mode, it not only writes the Boolean value of its test expression to the FIFO, but it reads the prior value from the FIFO (Figure 2.5). Then, one of four things can happen.

a)

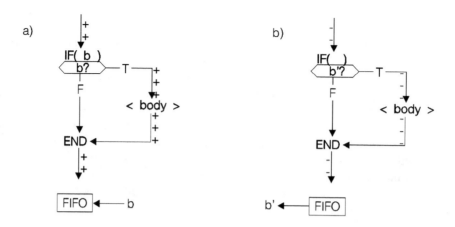

b)

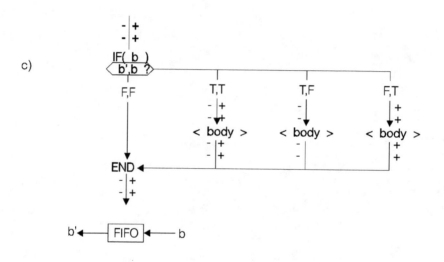

c)

Modes: SHOW   UPDATE   ERASE

Figure 2.5. The operation of the IF statement. (a) In SHOW mode, the Boolean value of the test is written to the FIFO and used to steer the conditional. (b) In ERASE mode, the old value of the test is read from the FIFO and used to steer the conditional. (c) In UPDATE mode, the new value is written to the FIFO, and the old value is read from it. If the two values are equal, one of them is used to steer the conditional. If they are unequal, the body is performed in SHOW mode if the new value is True; otherwise it is performed in ERASE mode.

If both values are TRUE, the body is executed (in UPDATE mode).

If both values are FALSE, the body is simply skipped.

If one of the values is TRUE and the other is FALSE, the body is executed regardless. If the *new* value is TRUE, the mode is set to SHOW (temporarily) and the body is executed.

If the *prior* value is TRUE, the mode is set to ERASE temporarily and the body is executed.

In this way, a change in the truth value of the test expression causes the graphics of its body text to be made visible or invisible.

If this sounds complicated, it is very easy to implement. We need two macros to form the IF statement and to END its body, along with a utility macro called PROTECT:

```
#define IF(test)\
        {int savemode = mode;\
                if (ifutil(PROTECT((test)&&1))){

#define END\
        } mode = savemode; }

#define PROTECT(expr) (mode & SHOW ? (expr) : 0)
```

Using these macros, the way we make something conditionally visible in the display procedure is to put it in the body of an IF–END construct:

```
IF( <visibility condition> )

    <primitives to be visible or not>

    END
```

The logic of the IF statement is buried in the function *ifutil*:

```
int ifutil(test) int test; {
        int oldtest;
        putgetInt(&test, &oldtest);
        if (mode==SHOW) return test;
        else if (mode==ERASE) return oldtest;
        else if (test==oldtest) return test;
        else {
                mode = (test ? SHOW : ERASE);
                return 1;
                }
        }
```

The reason we wrap the argument to *ifutil* in the PROTECT macro is that, in general, application-specific calculations should never be performed in ERASE mode. The reason we say *(test) && 1* rather than just *(test)* is because we are only interested in the truth or falsity of *test*.

Those who have studied theoretical computer science know that if a language has conditionals, subroutines, and the ability to manipulate data, it doesn't need any more to be a fully functional language. For example, if you want to program a loop, you can do it by writing a recursive subroutine that calls itself inside a conditional. However, in a practical sense this would be cumbersome, which is why languages have FOR and WHILE statements. Nevertheless, there is a close relationship between FOR and IF statements, making handling FOR statements easy in differential execution (Figure 2.6).

The macro to implement FOR is very simple:

```
#define FOR(init, test, increment )\
    { int savemode = mode;\
        for(PROTECT(init); PROTECT(test); PROTECT(increment)){
```

and it is used as follows:

```
FOR( i = 0, i < n, i++)

    < graphics to have n copies of >

    END
```

This END is the same macro that is used to close the IF statement. Notice that the only difference between this and a normal *for* statement is that its arguments are separated by commas rather than semicolons.

This is enough machinery to tackle a problem that used to be considered very

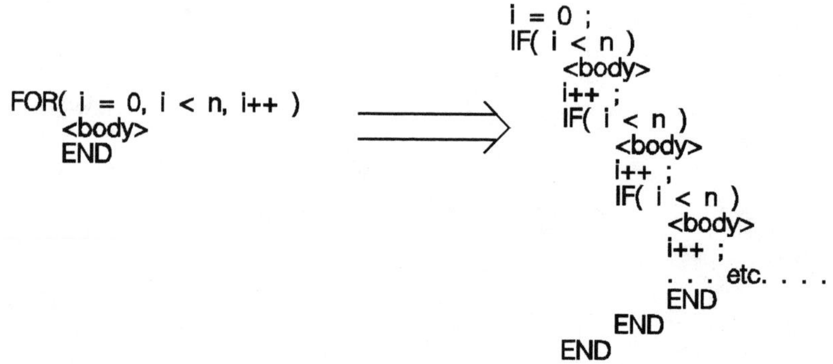

Figure 2.6. FOR is equivalent to a nested cascade of IF statements.

tough: the animated display of a binary tree. Assuming the tree structure has the following declaration:

```
struct node {
        struct node *left, *right;
        int value;
        };

struct node * ptop;
```

Its image can be maintained by the following compact display procedure:

```
view(){
        CALL(viewtree,(ptop, 320, 0, 320, 10, 160));
        }

viewtree(p, x0, y0, x, y, dx)
        struct node *p;
        int x0, y0, x, y, dx;
{
        IF(p)
                CALL(line,(x0, y0, x, y));
                CALL(text,(x, y, "%d", p->value));
                CALL(viewtree,(p->left, x, y, x-dx, y+10, dx/2));
                CALL(viewtree,(p->right, x, y, x+dx, y+10, dx/2));
                END
        }
```

The macro CALL is used inside a display procedure to call a subroutine of the display procedure. Its only purpose is to make sure that no arguments are evaluated in ERASE mode:

```
#define CALL(func, arglist)\
        (mode & SHOW ? (func arglist) : (func()))
```

The display procedure, since it automatically handles erasing as well as drawing, is really doing the work of three procedures: a *show_tree* procedure, an *update_tree* procedure, and an *erase_tree* procedure (Figure 2.7). Its value is that it eliminates the source code redundancy of having three procedures.

A single invocation of the display procedure in UPDATE mode can perform all erasing and drawing required to bring the image up-to-date, no matter how much the binary tree has changed since the prior invocation. For example, if the topmost node of the tree is deleted, the image requires substantial revision (Figure 2.8).

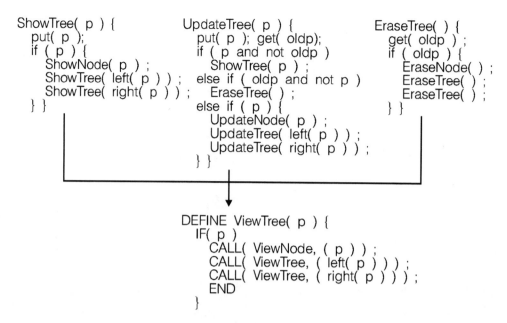

```
ShowTree( p ) {              UpdateTree( p ) {            EraseTree( ) {
    put( p );                    put( p ); get( oldp);        get( oldp ) ;
    if ( p ) {                   if ( p and not oldp )        if ( oldp ) {
        ShowNode( p ) ;              ShowTree( p ) ;              EraseNode( ) ;
        ShowTree( left( p ) ) ;  else if ( oldp and not p )       EraseTree( ) ;
        ShowTree( right( p ) ) ;     EraseTree( ) ;               EraseTree( ) ;
} }                              else if ( p ) {              } }
                                     UpdateNode( p ) ;
                                     UpdateTree( left( p ) ) ;
                                     UpdateTree( right( p ) ) ;
                                } }
```

```
DEFINE ViewTree( p ) {
    IF( p )
        CALL( ViewNode, ( p ) ) ;
        CALL( ViewTree, ( left( p ) ) ) ;
        CALL( ViewTree, ( right( p ) ) ) ;
    END
}
```

Figure 2.7. Under differential execution, one display procedure does the work of three.

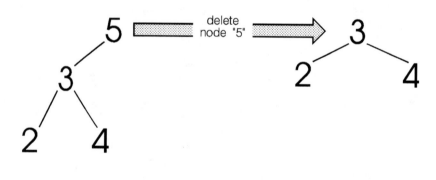

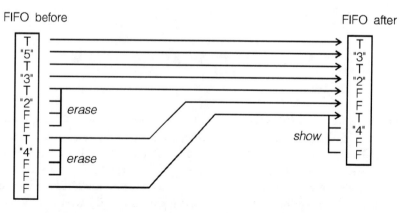

Figure 2.8. A single update of the image of a binary tree after deleting the topmost node. T and F represent binary values of IF expressions.

The performance of this technique is linear but has a good multiplicative constant. The time it takes to update a display, over and above any erasing and/or drawing, is proportional to the number of visible primitives. The technique, however, is fast due to its simplicity and the fact that it is compiled. For example, to update an image of a binary tree generally takes less than 500 instructions per visible node. On a 1-million-instruction-per-second processor, this is less than 16 milliseconds if the tree contains 32 visible nodes. Most modern computers have much higher clock speeds and so would perform the update that much more quickly.

Similarly, the storage used by the algorithm is only what it stores in the FIFO, which is around 20 bytes per node for the display procedure given above. For a 32-node tree, this gives 640 bytes—a miserly figure. In addition, there is no need for pointers, garbage collection, or any of the other complications associated with graphics based on data structures or OOP.

All of this discussion is predicated on our having a way to erase graphical primitives without damaging the image. A general solution to the problem of erasing objects that overlap one another called the *two-phase update method*, is given below. This is a complication on the update technique presented so far. However, before I present it, I should mention that it has seldom been needed. A sample program using two-phase update is given in Appendix D.

Many applications do not put overlapping objects on the screen, because to do so could obscure potentially important information. In such cases, it is acceptable to erase an object by redrawing it in the background color. In most other cases, the exclusive-OR method of erasing is acceptable.

When neither exclusive-OR nor background-color erasing is adequate to the need, the two-phase method can be used, but it is somewhat more complex. The two-phase method relies on keeping a record, for every visible primitive, containing the primitive's bounding rectangle, along with a damage marker. The basic idea is that there is an additional global variable, the *phase* having values 1 and 2. To update the image, the mode is set to UPDATE, and the display procedure is invoked twice, first with *phase* equal to 1, then with it equal to 2. If a primitive is going to do any erasing, it does it (by redrawing in the background color) in phase 1, and if it is going to do any drawing, it does it in phase 2. Whenever a primitive is erased or drawn, the bounding boxes of all overlapping primitives are marked as damaged. As a primitive is visited in the display sequence, its being damaged becomes a reason for it to be redrawn as shown in Figure 2.9.

The operation of the IF statement in two-phase update is difficult to explain but easy to program as shown in Figure 2.10.

Finally, in displaying dynamic images it may be objectionable to update the image live in front of the viewer's eyes. The *double-buffer technique* takes care of this by having two video frame buffers. While the image in one buffer is being updated, the viewer is watching the other buffer. When the update is complete, the buffers are electronically swapped, giving the illusion of instantaneous update.

The speed at which double-buffering can run depends on how quickly the offscreen buffer can be updated. It may be desirable to update it incrementally, for speed. The simplest way to accomplish this using differential execution is to start

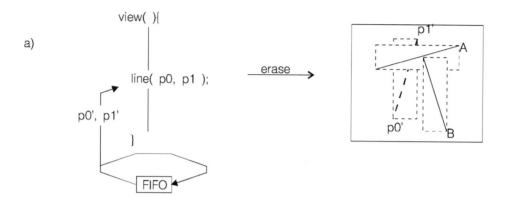

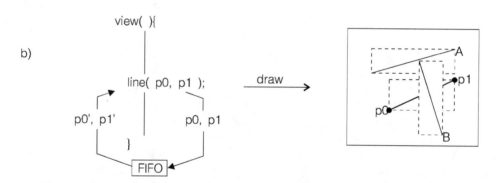

Figure 2.9. Handling overlap via a two-phase update. The line segment from p0 to p1 is to be obscured by line segments A and B. Points p0 and p1 change, causing the line segment from p0 to p1 to be erased and redrawn. The update is performed in two invocations of the display procedure, denoted UPDATE1 and UPDATE2. In the UPDATE1 phase (a) all erasing is done, and overlapping objects (line segment A) are marked as damaged. The prior values of p0 and p1 are cycled back into the FIFO, leaving the FIFO unchanged. In the UPDATE2 phase (b) all drawing is done, and again all overlapping objects (line segment B) are marked as damaged. Line segments A and B are later redrawn in the UPDATE2 phase because they have been marked as damaged.

```
int if_util( int b ){
    int b1;
    if ( mode == SHOW ){
        if ( phase == 2 ) putInt( b ) ;
        return b ;
    }
    else if ( mode == ERASE ){
        getInt( & b1 ) ;
        if ( phase == 1 ) putInt( b1 );
        return b1 ;
    }
    else /* mode == UPDATE */ {
        getInt( & b1 ) ;
        putInt( phase == 1 ? b1 : b ) ;
        if ( b == b1 ) return b ;
        mode = ( b ? SHOW : ERASE ) ;
        return 1 ;
    }
}
```

Figure 2.10. The IF utility function for 2-phase update. In both phases, the IF utility returns the same value as it does in single-phase update, so that the IF statement appears to behave the same in both phases. However, in phase 1, it leaves the FIFO unchanged by re-cycling the old Boolean value. This action is what enables phase 2 to also see the old Boolean value.

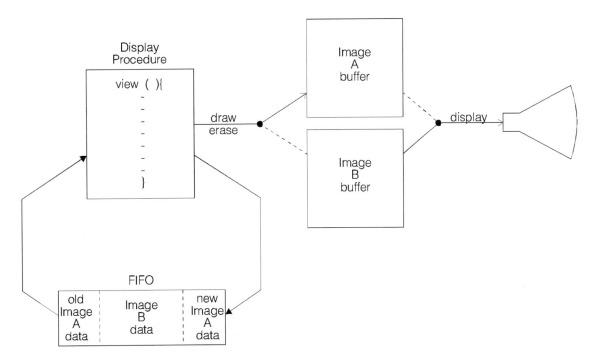

Figure 2.11. Double-buffered display maintenance. The display is driven from one buffer while the other buffer is being incrementally updated. After each invocation of the display procedure, the buffers are electronically swapped. The process is started by invoking the display procedure twice in SHOW mode, so that the FIFO contains parameters for the images in both buffers.

off the display history with two SHOW invocations instead of one (Figure 2.11). By doing so, the FIFO contains data for two buffers.

Here is a simple implementation of difex:

```
 1 /* difex.h  differential execution support */
 2
 3 #ifndef _DIFEX_H
 4 #define _DIFEX_H
 5
 6 #define DE_QSIZ 4096
 7
 8 #ifdef IN_DIFEX
 9 int deMode;
10 unsigned int deEnq, deDeq;
11 char deQueue[DE_QSIZ];
12 #else
13 extern int deMode;
14 extern unsigned int deEnq, deDeq;
15 extern char deQueue[];
16 #endif
17
18 #define DE_ERASE  1
19 #define DE_SHOW   2
20 #define DE_UPDATE 3
21
22 #define PROTECT(expr)(deMode!=DE_ERASE ? (expr) : 0)
23
24 #define IF(test){\
25     int svmode=deMode;\
26     if(IfUtil(PROTECT(test)&&1)){
27
28 #define END } deMode=svmode;}
29
30 #define FOR(init,test,incr){\
31     int svmode=deMode;\
32     for(PROTECT(init);PROTECT(test)&&1;PROTECT(incr)){
33
34 #define CALL(fn,arglist)(deMode!=DE_ERASE ? (fn arglist) : (fn))
35
36 #define SWITCH(v){\
37     int svmode = deMode;\
38     int demode0 = deMode;\
39     int demode1 = deMode;\
40     int swval[4];\
41     swval[DE_SHOW] = PROTECT(v);\
42     swval[DE_UPDATE] = swval[DE_SHOW];\
43     GetPut(&swval[DE_ERASE], &swval[DE_SHOW], sizeof(int));\
44     if (svMode==DE_UPDATE && swval[DE_ERASE]!=swval[DE_SHOW]){\
45             demode0 = DE_ERASE;\
46             demode1 = DE_SHOW;\
47             }\
48     for(deMode=demode0; deMode<=demode1; deMode++)\
49             switch(swval[deMode]){
50
51 extern void GetPut(char* g, char* p, int len);
```

```
52
53 extern void GetPutStr(char* g, char* p);
54
55 #endif /* _DIFEX_H */
56
```

In the file *difex.h*, line 6 defines the size of the FIFO queue. Lines 8–16 define the queue structure itself and the global mode variable *deMode*.

The three mode values, *DE_ERASE, DE_SHOW,* and *DE_UPDATE* are given in lines 18–20. The values 1, 2, and 3 are chosen to simplify some of the processing.

The *PROTECT(expr)* macro is given in line 22. Its purpose is to protect expressions from being evaluated in ERASE mode.

The *IF(test)* and *END* macros are given in lines 24–28. They save and restore the mode. The body is executed by an *if* statement based on the return value of function *IfUtil(test)*. The test expression is protected against being evaluated in ERASE mode, and it is turned into a Boolean 1 or 0 by the operation *&&1*.

The *FOR* statement macro is given in lines 30–32. It is implemented in a way very similar to the *IF* statement.

Line 34 defines the *CALL(fn, arglist)* macro. Its purpose is to let you call a subroutine within differential execution. It protects the subroutine's arguments from being evaluated in ERASE mode. Unfortunately, this type of macro cannot be used with ANSI-style argument list type checking, but that is a small price to pay.

If we can have a single-branch *IF* statement, why not a two-branch conditional? I couldn't think of a good way to do it, other than to go all the way to an N-branch conditional, the *SWITCH* statement macro given in lines 36–49. If you want an *IF t THEN a ELSE b* construct, you can write it as:

```
SWITCH(t)
default:
        a;
case 0:
        b;
        END
```

The way it works is to have a switch statement enclosed in a *for* loop to execute it either once or twice. If the ambient mode is *UPDATE* and the test value has changed, the body is executed first in *ERASE* mode with the old test value and then in *SHOW* mode with the new test value.

```
1 /* difex.c  differential execution support */
2
```

```
 3 #define IN_DIFEX
 4 #include "difex.h"
 5
 6 void GetPut(char* g, char* p, int len){
 7     int i;
 8     if (deMode != DE_SHOW){
 9             for (i=0; i<len; i++){
10                     g[i] = deQueue[deDeq++];
11                     if (deDeq >= DE_QSIZ) deDeq = 0;
12                     }
13             }
14     if (deMode != DE_ERASE){
15             for (i=0; i<len; i++){
16                     deQueue[deEnq++] = p[i];
17                     if (deEnq >= DE_QSIZ) deEnq = 0;
18                     }
19             }
20     }
21
22 void GetPutStr(char* g, char* p){
23     int c;
24     if (deMode != DE_SHOW){
25             while(1){
26                     c = (*g++) = deQueue[deDeq++];
27                     if (deDeq >= DE_QSIZ) deDeq = 0;
28                     if (c==0) break;
29                     }
30             }
31     if (deMode != DE_ERASE){
32             while (1){
33                     c = deQueue[deEnq++] = (*p++);
34                     if (deEnq >= DE_QSIZ) deEnq = 0;
35                     if (c==0) break;
36                     }
37             }
38     }
39
40 int IfUtil(int test){
41     int oldtest;
42     int rval = test;
43     GetPut((char*)&oldtest, (char*)&test, sizeof(test));
44     if (deMode==DE_SHOW)
45             rval = test;
46     else if (deMode==DE_UPDATE){
47             if (test==oldtest)
48                     rval = test;
49             else {
50                     deMode = (test ? DE_SHOW : DE_ERASE);
51                     rval = 1;
52                     }
53             }
54     else
55             rval = oldtest;
56     return rval;
57     }
```

This file defines the executable functions needed to run differential execution. The function *GetPut* (lines 6–20) is used for both getting and putting data items of known size in the queue. It takes the correct action depending on the mode. The reason it performs the get before the put is so that if the same variable is used for both input and output, it will put the same value that it gets, which can be useful for long-term storage of values.

Lines 22–38 define the function *GetPutStr*, which is used for getting and putting null-terminated character strings (which can vary in size). Warning: The buffer that you get the string into has to be big enough to accommodate the length of the string.

The function *IfUtil(test)* is given in lines 40–56. Assuming *test* is either 0 or 1, it gets the old value and puts the new value (conditioned on the mode). Based on the mode and on the old and new test values, it may change the mode, and it returns 0 or 1 to control the *IF* statement that is calling it.

CONCLUSION

Data can be redundant, meaning that you have to update it in multiple places to keep it consistent. Source code can also be redundant, if you have to update it in multiple places to keep it consistent.

In ordinary programming, data redundancy is a primary reason for source code redundancy, because the source code must call for each of the data updates. Source code redundancy is *bad* because programmers are fallible, and the more places that require changes to the source code, the more bugs will be introduced. A way to attack this problem is to find ways to maintain redundant data while minimizing exposure to programmers' mistakes. That is the issue being addressed by differential methods.

In the case of display maintenance, we see a recurring theme: language replacing data. Differential execution provides a little language for stating what display is to be visible. This language has a technically interesting control structure. As in the case of the redesigned CIM simulation, the focus shifted away from run-time data and objects toward the development-time language. The purpose of this shift is to make it easier to change the program code as requirements change.

3

Language

College curriculum in computer science generally includes one fairly rigorous course on compiler technology, and there may also be some exposure to the writing of interpreters. The student often comes away feeling that these are fairly isolated and arcane subjects.

I would like to see the emphasis change. The skills of designing and implementing special-purpose languages should be broadened and treated as general problem-solving techniques, not as a narrow specialty. I feel this way because (in my experience) most successful large software systems contain one or more linguistic components, either an interpreted macro language, some sort of code generator, a parser, a symbol table, or whatever. Skill in these areas is often a mark of a productive senior developer.

As an example, the other day I was attending a class on performance tuning for a popular client-server database system. The server translates user procedures into an internal interpreted instruction set. These procedures are not re-entrant, however, a fact that hurts performance when queries overlap. For a developer skilled in building interpreters, re-entrancy is a trivial capability to provide. (To provide it, it is necessary only that interpreted procedures be read-only.)

There is a valid point of view that the last thing the world needs is yet another computer language. The learning of new languages has to be funded by somebody, and what's wrong with the old languages anyway? It's bad enough that the labor pool grows obsolete as quickly as it does, without helping this along.

The other side of the argument is that there is a software crisis. The current state-of-the-art software is not up to the demands being placed on it. Typical software is too big, too slow, unreliable, too expensive, and resistant to change. Shouldn't we try to do better? I believe that this is as much a technical problem as it is a people problem. We need to have good solid techniques that really work, and we need to train people to use them. I don't see any alternative. That is what this book is about.

(There are those who hold that object-oriented programming points the way out of the mess. I think OOP is a fine idea, but I believe this hope is a false one, for reasons I will elaborate later.)

I will try to explain why better software necessarily involves linguistic techniques.

Point 1: Users of software care about documents, accounts, scientific data, business data, games, industrial processes—the subject matter that the software enlivens for them. They do not care about classes, repositories, memory structures, process, interrupt handlers, structured programming, or any of the other technology of software.

Point 2: Software is built because users want it, and they change their minds, often.

Point 3: A developer stands with one foot in the user world and one foot in the software world. Developers have to translate between the problem as stated in a user's terms and the solution as stated in an implementation language.

Conclusion: The more closely this implementation language *resembles* the user's statement of the problem, the easier it will be to change the implementation when the user redefines the problem.

This concept of resemblance between languages can easily be made objective. When the *mdiff* program compares two files, at the end it reports the number N of differences it found. If a piece of software is modified to accommodate a single user requirement, and the before-and-after source files are compared, N is a simple measure of the relative difficulty of the modification. *To the extent that N is minimized, on the average, I say the software is stated in a problem-oriented language (POL).*

N is a direct measure of the redundancy of the source code with respect to individual requirements. This redundancy should be minimized because it provides the opportunity for errors. If the programmer performs modifications to the text correctly 90 percent of the time, *he or she will be inserting bugs at a rate proportional to N*. When source code is structured so that N approaches the limit of one difference per requirement, it must necessarily take on a structural if not literal resemblance to the user's statement of the problem, which is why I say it is *problem-oriented*. I do not define the term *problem-oriented* in terms of surface syntax or implementation techniques, but in terms of keyboard events precipitated by requirements.

It is worthwhile to compare the measure N against other software complexity measures. N is more related to development-time events than it is to run-time data or control structure as are the cyclomatic measures. N includes specifications, documentation, build instructions, test instructions, and other ancillary data under the complexity umbrella, if those files are included in the source control system. The measure firmly defines the goal (minimizing average N) over software lifetime, as opposed to a measure such as "thousand lines of code" (KLOC), where it is unclear even whether less or more code is to be desired.

SIMPLE INTERPRETED LANGUAGES

Often a program can be simplified by storing its internal data in the form of an interpreted instruction set, rather than as a linked-list data structure. When this is done, that instruction set becomes a problem-oriented language. For example, computer graphic images can be represented with simple byte-coded opcode streams as well as with linked lists of data blocks. The byte codes are usually much more compact and amenable to adding advanced features such as subroutines, and easier to save and restore from files.

The following code is an interpreter for a simple LOGO-like language for making line drawings. The idea is that there is a "turtle" having a position and orientation on the X-Y plane. The one-letter command "f" causes the turtle to move forward one unit of distance, leaving a colored line, and the command "l" causes it to turn left, in place, by an angle of 15 degrees. The parentheses characters "(" and ")" delimit a *subroutine*, a string of commands that can be repeated later by using the "c" command. So, for example, the string:

```
(fflllllll)ccc
```

causes the creation of a square having two units on a side. The interpreter is as follows:

```
 1 /* interp.c  simple LOGO-like graphical interpreter */
 2
 3 #include <stdio.h>
 4 #include "..\fastmath\fastmath.h"
 5 #include <graph.h>  /* for graphics */
 6
 7 #define SCREENWIDTH 640
 8 #define SCREENHEIGHT 350
 9
10 void myline(FIXP x, FIXP y, FIXP newx, FIXP newy){
11     _moveto(SCREENWIDTH/2 + TOLONG(x), SCREENHEIGHT/2 - TOLONG(y));
12     _lineto(SCREENWIDTH/2 + TOLONG(newx), SCREENHEIGHT/2 - TOLONG(newy));
13     }
14
15     /* the turtle's state */
16 FIXP x, y;
17 int theta;  /* in degrees */
18     /* distance to move forward */
19 FIXP dis = TOFIXP(10);
20     /* the command buffer */
21 char buf[1024];
22     /* temporary position variables */
23 FIXP newx, newy;
```

```
24
25 /* interp(pc): interpret commands starting at pc (program counter) */
26 void interp(char * pc){
27     int level;         /* temporary used for scanning over subroutine */
28     char *subpc = NULL;
29     /* for each command character up to right paren or null */
30     while(*pc) switch(*pc++){
31             break; case 'f':
32                     newx = x + FIXTIMES(fcos(theta),dis);
33                     newy = y + FIXTIMES(fsin(theta),dis);
34                     myline(x,y,newx,newy);
35                     x = newx; y = newy;
36             break; case 'l':
37                     theta += 15;
38             break; case '(':
39                     subpc = pc;
40                     for (level=1; *pc && level>0; pc++){
41                             if (*pc=='(') level++;
42                             else if (*pc==')') level--;
43                             }
44                     interp(subpc);
45             break; case ')':
46                     return;
47             break; case 'c':
48                     if (subpc!=NULL)
49                             interp(subpc);
50             }
51     }
52
53 void main(int argc, char *argv[]){
54     argc--; argv++;
55     if (argc<=0){
56             printf("Usage: interp <command string>\n");
57             return;
58             }
59     strcpy(buf, argv[0]);
60     _setvideomode(_ERESCOLOR);
61     _setcolor(15);
62     interp(buf);
63     /* printf("Press any key to continue..."); /**/
64     getch();
65     _setvideomode(_DEFAULTMODE);
66     }
```

Line 4 includes *fastmath.h* (explained in Appendix A), a fixed point fraction math package that I use instead of floating point, for speed. Fixed point fraction variables are of type FIXP, which is a 32-bit integer in which the 10 low-order bits are considered the fractional part.

Line 5 includes the *graph.h*, the header file for the Microsoft library of simple graphic routines used for graphical output.

Lines 10–13 define *myline*, a routine to draw a line. The routine calls the necessary library routines. It uses a coordinate system centered on the screen with +Y going toward the top of the screen.

Lines 16–17 give the state of the "turtle," in the form of an <x,y> location, and a heading angle *theta* in degrees.

Line 21 defines the buffer *buf* where the command string resides while it is being interpreted.

The interpreter function itself starts at line 25. Its argument is a pointer to the first character at which to begin interpreting. It is a *while* loop containing a *switch* on the current opcode character. If the opcode is "f" (forward) it draws a line and moves the turtle to the end of the line. If the opcode is "l" (left turn) it adds 15 degrees to the turtle's heading angle.

The subroutine syntax consists of parentheses "(" and ")" surrounding the opcodes belonging to the subroutine. For this simple example, the semantics are that there can be only one subroutine currently defined, so it need not have a name, and you call the subroutine with the "c" command. Also, when the subroutine is defined, it is also called once, so that using the code "(...)c" results in two invocations of the subroutine.

To implement subroutines you need three operations: defining, calling, and returning. The left parenthesis operation "(" causes a subroutine to be defined. This consists of remembering where the start of the subroutine is in variable *subpc*, and then scanning the program counter *pc* forward over the closing right parenthesis (lines 38–43). Since I decided that a subroutine should be called as soon as it is defined (so as to get at least one invocation of it), that takes place in line 44. The subroutine call operation "c" causes the subroutine to be invoked by passing its start address to a recursive invocation of *interp* (lines 47–49). The subroutine return operation ")" works simply by causing the interpreter to return (lines 45–46).

To invoke the interpreter you put the string of commands into the buffer and do *interp(buf)*. You can easily see how to add sophistication to this language. For example, you could add digit-processing to make numbers, which you could push on a stack to use as arguments for the commands. You could add opcodes such as "+" and "*" to do calculation on a stack. You could have a repeat operator "r," which could repeatedly execute the current subroutine some number of times. You could add register variables, in which to save and restore numbers, and subroutine pointers. You could make a simple IF statement by having a subroutine repeat either zero or one time. All these features can be added very easily and all should work correctly on the first or second try. Interpreters tend to be very low-redundancy programs.

Of course, this example is clearly just a "toy." But the point is that constructing an interpreter capable of serious work would not be much more involved than creating the one in the example. An example of a serious interpreted language is the format string in the C functions *printf* and *scanf*. Commercial software products often contain interpreters to achieve user-configurability. (Some examples are Lotus 1-2-3, Procomm communications software, and just about all text editors.) By going to full binary opcodes rather than only ASCII characters, a full instruction set can be developed, but then you may need a parser and printer to translate from human-readable syntax to opcodes and back.

These are the choices to be weighed, but in any case they are alternatives to data structure, which must also be interpreted.

LOOKAHEAD AND INVARIANT RELATIONS

The theme being developed here is that when implementations start looking like problem statements, we can say they are stated in a problem-oriented language. Such a language can occur without any particular linguistic technology, such as parsing, and it can be the result of nothing more than a particular organization of the source code.

One-item lookahead is a technique familiar to experienced programmers. It is applicable in just about any kind of program that processes a sequential input stream, such as records being read from a sequential file or characters being read from a keyboard. In such an input stream there usually are subdivisions, or *control breaks* in EDP jargon. For example, in reading a file of general ledger records sorted by major and minor account codes (Figure 3.1), production of summary totals at the end of each minor and major account is often desired.

Invariant Relations are little rules that you decide to follow within a program regarding the interrelationships of its data. Often the names of operations and variables are chosen so as to express these. (For example, if there is an array of items being used as a stack, rather than having a variable called *stack_pointer*, you would have a variable called *number_of_items*, and make sure that it always means what it says. This invariant relation eliminates nasty little confusions such as: Does the array start at 0 or 1, or do we pre-increment or post-increment when pushing and popping? In a totalizing program, one kind of invariant relation you might choose is, for example, that the aggregate of all totalizing variables, added together, equals the total of all amounts read in so far. This implies that as soon as you transfer a total you clear it.

Totalizing programs, while conceptually simple, often are complex because you don't know when you have finished with one account until you've read the first record of the next one. What you would like is the ability to look ahead one record in the input stream. If the next record is not a member of the current account, you would like to print your summaries before reading that record, not after (Figure 3.2). The way to do this is to have a global record buffer with an occupancy flag.

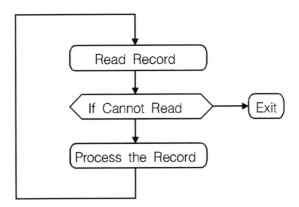

Figure 3.1. Traditional record processing.

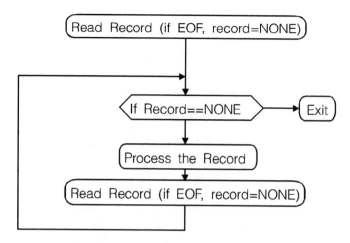

Figure 3.2. Lookahead record processing.

You form an invariant relation by saying to yourself: "The record in the global buffer is the next one in the input stream. I haven't really read it in yet. It's just there so I can look at it. If I like it, I will accept it."

Instead of reading a record in order to look at it, you simply look at it in the global buffer. If the occupancy flag is true, meaning there is a record occupying the buffer, and if the record belongs to the current account, then the record's numbers can be absorbed into the current account totals, and you can *accept* it as belonging to the current account. If the record is not in the buffer, or if it is there but does not belong to the current account, then the end of the current account has been reached, so summaries can be printed, and the global record is left alone. The operation of accepting a record consists of reading the following record into the global buffer (or clearing the occupancy flag if there are no more records).

To make this work, it is necessary to do an initial read of one record, to "prime the pump," so that the invariant is true on entering the main loop(s). It also means that, rather than reading a record *before* looking at it, you read the record *after* looking at it. Since this strikes some as rather odd, that is why the operation is called *accept* rather than *read*.

To see how this works, suppose we have a file of expense records ordered by major and minor account numbers. Each record could have a structure such as this:

```
struct my_record_struct {
    int major;   /* major account number */
    int minor;   /* minor account number */
    int amount;  /* expense amount */
    };
```

Conceptually, the file has a simple nested structure. For example, it could have been generated by a program with pseudocode:

```
For each major account
    For each minor account in major account
        For each expense in major/minor account
            Print an expense record
```

According to the linguistic methodology, a program to read the file ought to be able to have a similar structure. Without using lookahead, however, the program would look like this:

```
Clear grand total, major account total, minor account total

Repeat
    Read a record
    If there is none to read, repeat exit

    If there was previous record & this record
    is not in the same major/minor account
        Print the minor account total
        Add minor acct total to major acct
        Clear minor acct total

    If there was previous record & this record
    is not in the same major account
        Print the major account total
        Add major acct total to grand total
        Clear major acct total.

    Add record's amount to minor acct total

    end of repeat block

If any record at all was read
    Print minor account total
    Add minor acct total to major acct total
    Print major acct total
    Add major account total to grand total

    Print grand total
```

The non-lookahead program is quite different from the conceptual structure of the input file. It is redundant because the code to print and accumulate minor and major totals appears twice. Correctness is difficult to verify. For example, to be certain that each record's amount is accumulated in the total for its minor and major accounts requires carefully following the logic of the two big IF statements inside the loop.

Using lookahead, the program looks like this:

```
Prime the pump: read initial record
Clear grand total

/* FOREACH MAJOR ACCOUNT */
While there is a next record
    Get major account number from record
    Clear major account total

    /* FOREACH MINOR ACCOUNT */
    While next record belongs to major account
        Get minor account number from record
        Clear minor account total

        /* FOREACH EXPENSE RECORD IN MINOR ACCT */
        While next rec belongs major/minor acct
            /* PROCESS THE EXPENSE RECORD */
            Add rec amount to minor acct total
            Accept the record

        Print total for minor acct
        Add minor acct total to major acct total

    Print total for major account
    Add major account total to grand total

Print grand total
```

The overall structure of the program is the same as the conceptual description of the file, embellished with code to accumulate and print totals.

Correctness is easier to verify. Observe that the inner loop accepts only records belonging to one minor account, and records are accepted nowhere else in the code. (Why doesn't the preliminary read count?) Since the inner-loop total is cleared before entering the loop and printed only once upon exiting the loop, and each record's amount is added to the total just before acceptance of that record, each record is accumulated once and only once, and is accumulated to its own minor account total. Similar reasoning applies to the higher-level loops.

Proofs of program correctness are generally considered an arcane academic pursuit, but in fact, are not a bad idea in normal programming. The procedure for proving correctness is that some Doubting Thomas asks embarassing questions that you have to try and answer:

Could an empty file cause something to go wrong? If the file is empty, the sequence of execution is:

```
Prime the pump: do initial read
        (which fails to set occupancy flag)
Clear grand total
While there is a next record
        (there isn't, so loop iterates 0 times)
Print grand total
        (which is zero)
```

So it prints a total of zero, which is correct.

Could a file of only one record create wrong output? If there is only one record, the priming read will get it and set the occupancy flag. Then the major account loop will see that the record is there and will enter its first iteration, but will not accept the record. However, the loop will take note of the major account number from the record (and clear the major account total). The minor account loop sees that the record is there and sees that the record's major account number is the same as the current major account number and so clears its minor total and takes note of the minor account number. The expense record loop sees the record and sees that the record belongs to the current major and minor account numbers, so the loop enters its first iteration. It adds the expense amount to the minor total and accepts the record. Since there are no more records, this leaves the occupancy flag false. On trying the second iteration of the expense loop, there is no record, so the loop terminates. The total for the minor account, consisting of only the one amount, is printed and added to the major account total. Likewise the minor account loop terminates, and the major account total, consisting of only the one record amount, is printed and added to the grand total. Likewise the major account loop terminates, and the grand total is printed, consisting of only the one record amount. The result is three totals—minor, major, and grand—each consisting of the amount on the one record.

Could a record be totalled twice? Because each record can be accepted only once (by the definition of "accept"), and because the only place a record is accepted is in the statement following the adding of its amount to the minor total, then if a record was added to the minor total, it must have been accepted, and vice versa (barring catastrophic failures). Could that record's amount, once it is in the minor total, show up more than once in the major total? After the minor total is added to the major total (in the only statement that does so), before that addition statement is reached again, control has to pass through the prior statement that clears the minor total (because there is no other way to get there), so the amount will not be accumulated twice. The same argument holds for the relationship between the major total and the grand total.

Could a record not be totalled? Since any given record is accepted once, and it is accepted on the line following the addition of its amount to the minor total, it is accumulated into the minor total. Could the minor total fail to be added to the major total? After exiting the expense loop, the minor total is completely accumulated. At that point it is printed and added to the major loop. There is no place else that control could go (barring catastrophic failure). Thus the minor total is accumulated into the major total. Likewise, the major total is accumulated into the grand total.

Could a total be cleared when it should not have been? The minor total is supposed to consist of the total of the expense records in that major/minor account. All and only those records are accumulated and accepted in the expense record loop. The minor total is cleared before entering that loop, and that is the only statement where it is cleared. Therefore, whenever the minor total is cleared, it is cleared prior to forming a sum of expense records for the major/minor account, and that is the proper time. Thus the minor total cannot be cleared at an improper time. Likewise for the higher-level totals.

Could a total not be cleared when it should? A total should be cleared before performing the loop that accumulates it. Thus, if a loop executes that accumulates a total, the total must have been cleared, because the clearing statement came right before the loop, and there is no other way to reach the loop.

I have witnessed experienced COBOL programmers treating the lookahead technique as a mysterious productivity secret, the mark of the *cognoscenti*. It isn't generally taught to introductory classes. Why not?

A USEFUL LEXICAL ANALYZER

In the next section, I will show how to write useful parsers without any special tools; this will be much easier, however, if we first write a subroutine called a *lexical analyzer*, embodied in a routine called *lexan()*. Its job is to accept just enough characters from the input stream to get a single meaningful token, such as a number, identifier, or punctuation mark, while ignoring any whitespace or comments. It will leave the result in a global variable called *token*, declared like this:

```
 1 /* lexan.h a general purpose lexical analyzer */
 2
 3 #ifdef IN_LEXAN
 4 #define DEFVAR(typ,name) typ name
 5 #else
 6 #define DEFVAR(typ,name) extern typ name
 7 #endif
 8
 9 DEFVAR(int, token);
10 #define T_ID  1
11 #define T_LONG 2
12 DEFVAR(long, token_long);
13 DEFVAR(char, tokstr[128]);
14
15 extern int lex_getc();      /* user must define this routine */
16                             /* it should return next char or EOF */
17
18 extern void init_lexan();   /* call before parsing. reads 1st token */
19 extern void lexan();        /* read next token into global vars */
20
21 #define SEE(s)(token==T_ID && strcmp(tokstr,(s))==0)
22
23 #undef DEFVAR
24
```

The routine is fairly simple. There are two global variables c, and $c1$. c holds a character, and it is a one-character lookahead into the input stream. $c1$ is its prior value, so that we can check for combinations like /*. There is a macro GETC whose job is to accept the current character by getting the next character of input into c.

The job of *lexan()*, assuming that *c* contains the one-character lookahead, is to first accept all whitespace and comments up to the next token, and then to accept the characters of the token, which is either an identifier, number, punctuation mark, or end-of-file EOF. You can easily see how to enhance it by putting in strings, floating point numbers, and so on.

```
1 /* lexan.c  a general purpose lexical analyzer */
2
3 #ifndef EOF
4 #define EOF (-1)
5 #endif
6
7 #define IN_LEXAN
8 #include "lexan.h"
9
10 static int c;
11 static int c1;
12
13 #define GETC (c1 = c, c = lex_getc())
14
15 #define MAXLONG 0x7fffffffL
16
17 static long maxacc[10] = {
18      (MAXLONG - 0)/10,
19      (MAXLONG - 1)/10,
20      (MAXLONG - 2)/10,
21      (MAXLONG - 3)/10,
22      (MAXLONG - 4)/10,
23      (MAXLONG - 5)/10,
24      (MAXLONG - 6)/10,
25      (MAXLONG - 7)/10,
26      (MAXLONG - 8)/10,
27      (MAXLONG - 9)/10,
28      };
29
30 #define ISALPHA(c)\
31      (((c)>='a' && (c)<='z') || ((c)>='A' && (c)<='Z') || ((c)=='_'))
32
33 #define ISDIGIT(c) ((c)>='0' && (c)<='9')
34
35 void init_lexan(){
36     c = c1 = 0;
37     GETC;
38     lexan();
39     }
40
41 void lexan(){
42     /* first accept comments and whitespace */
43     while(1){
44             /* accept whitespace */
45             while(c!=EOF && c<=' ') GETC;
46             /* if next char is slash */
47             if (c=='/'){
48                     /* get the char following */
49                     GETC;
50                     /* if star, it's one kind of comment */
```

```
 51                                    if (c=='*'){
 52                                            GETC;
 53                                            while(c!=EOF){
 54                                                    if (c1=='*' && c=='/'){
 55                                                            GETC;
 56                                                            break;
 57                                                            }
 58                                                    GETC;
 59                                                    }
 60                                            }
 61                                    /* if slash, it's other kind of comment */
 62                                    else if (c=='/'){
 63                                            GETC;
 64                                            while(!(c==EOF || c=='\n' || c=='\r'))
 65                                                    GETC;
 66                                            }
 67                                    /* else token is '/', so return it */
 68                                    else {
 69                                            token = c1;
 70                                            return;
 71                                            }
 72                                    } /* possible start of comment */
 73                            /* if not comment, it's start of token */
 74                            else
 75                                    break;
 76                            } /* loop over whitespace */
 77            /* if it's numeric */
 78            if (ISDIGIT(c)){
 79                    long accum = 0;
 80                    while(ISDIGIT(c)){
 81                            /* watch out for overflow */
 82                            if (accum <= maxacc[c - '0']){
 83                                    accum = accum * 10 + (c - '0');
 84                                    }
 85                            GETC;
 86                            }
 87                    token_long = accum;
 88                    token = T_LONG;
 89                    }
 90            /* else if it's alphabetic */
 91            else if (ISALPHA(c)){
 92                    int n = 0;
 93                    /* get alphanumeric id */
 94                    while(ISALPHA(c)||ISDIGIT(c)){
 95                            if (n < sizeof(tokstr) - 1 ){
 96                                    tokstr[n++] = c;
 97                                    }
 98                            GETC;
 99                            }
100                    tokstr[n] = 0;
101                    token = T_ID;
102                    }
103            /* else it is a punctuation mark or EOF */
104            else {
105                    token = c;
106                    GETC;
107                    }
108    }
```

Imagine what would happen if this routine did not use one-character lookahead. Suppose tokens have no whitespace between them, as in "*qsort;*". In the process of accepting the token *qsort* it would have to read in the character ";" before knowing that the identifier *qsort* was complete. Then, when it came around to get the next token, the semicolon would be missed because it had already been read in. One way around this would be to have some sort of *ungetc* that could reverse the effect of reading a character. Personally, I have found it cleaner and more reliable to use lookahead than to try reversing the input (although I have used full backtracking on occasion).

LL(1) PARSERS

LL(1) parsers, also called *recursive-descent* parsers [Aho, Ullman '79] are very impressive-sounding, but represent a very simple, easily applied, and powerful technique. LL(1) parsers may be used when there is a need to process a character stream having a very flexible or nested structure.

In any string-language parser, there typically are two levels of interest, the *lexical* level, and the *grammatical* level. The lexical level is concerned with collecting individual characters and grouping them into meaningful tokens, such as identifiers, numbers, and punctuation marks, and with skipping over noise like whitespace and comments. The grammatical level, in turn, collects tokens in combinations representing meaningful groups and does meaningful things with them.

There exists a whole range of parsing techniques. LL(1) parsers are top-down in the sense that they have a good idea of what the structure is before looking at the input. The LR(1) or bottom-up parsers can handle languages that LL(1) parsers cannot. In the C language, for example, there are constructions difficult to handle with LL(1), such as the fact that either value expressions or datatype expressions can be nested inside parentheses, or that you can't tell if something is an array until you see the "[...]" at the far end of it. On the other hand, a language like COBOL is better handled with a backtracking type of top-down parser, because it has no distinct lexical token layer. The character-by-character syntax of record field definitions, for example, is very different from the syntax of the procedure section, and the syntax of statements is tricky (as in "ADD X AND Y TO Z GIVING Q"). The choice of parsing technique is affected by all these factors, but if you are designing your own language you can make sure the grammar is no more difficult than the problem requires. In these cases, LL(1) is often the best choice because of its simplicity and ease of modification.

Each time *lexan* is called, it uses lookahead at the character level to accept just enough characters to make a single token. It accepts as much leading whitespace and commentary as necessary, including none. It could have been called "read_token," but since it is being used in a lookahead manner, a better name for it might have been "accept token."

The *grammatical* routines depend on the application. They simply accept tokens in the desired combinations and do whatever should be done with them. Technically, the allowable groupings of tokens are called grammar rules, and can be described in a formal syntax. However, the advantage of an LL(1) parser is that it can be written as a series of routines that have the same structure as the grammar rules, so there isn't much to be gained by writing the rules separately.

As an example, here is a simple calculator program having infix expression syntax. Each routine is preceded by the formal grammar rule that it implements. The calculation is performed within the parser as the tokens are being accepted.

```
1  /* parse.c  simple LL(1) expression parser */
2
3  #include <stdio.h>
4  #include "..\lexan\lexan.h"
5
6  char testbuf[] = "7-5*2;";
7
8  char * pc = testbuf;
9
10 int lex_getc(){
11     if (*pc==0)
12             return EOF;
13     else
14             return *pc++;
15     }
16
17 int err = 0;
18
19 #define E if (err) return
20
21 void parseExpression(long *p);
22
23 void parsePrimitive(long *p){
24     err = 0;
25     if (token==T_LONG){
26             *p = token_long;
27             lexan();
28             }
29     else if (token=='-'){
30             lexan();
31             parsePrimitive(p);
32             *p = - *p;
33             }
34     else if (token=='('){
35             lexan();
36             parseExpression(p);
37             if (token == ')')
38                     lexan();
39             else
40                     err = 1;
41             }
42     else
43             err = 1;
44     }
45
46 void parseProduct(long *p){
47     long temp = 0;
48     err = 0;
```

```
49        parsePrimitive(p); E;
50        while(token=='/' || token=='*'){
51               int op = token;
52               lexan();
53               parsePrimitive(&temp); E;
54               if (op=='*') *p *= temp;
55               else if (op=='/') *p /= temp;
56               }
57        }
58
59 void parseSum(long *p){
60        long temp = 0;
61        err = 0;
62        parseProduct(p); E;
63        while(token=='+' || token=='-'){
64               int op = token;
65               lexan();
66               parseProduct(&temp); E;
67               if (op=='+') *p += temp;
68               else if (op=='-') *p -= temp;
69               }
70        }
71
72 void parseExpression(long *p){
73        err = 0;
74        parseSum(p);
75        }
76
77 void main(){
78        long temp = -1;
79        init_lexan();
80        parseExpression(&temp);
81        printf("%ld\n", temp);
82        if (err) printf("Err = %d\n", err);
83        }
```

Let's follow the operation of the calculator on a simple expression:

```
            7 - 5 * 2;

execution trace:          unaccepted tokens:

call parse_expression     7 - 5 * 2 ;
 call parse_sum           7 - 5 * 2 ;
  call parse_product      7 - 5 * 2 ;
   call parse_primitive   7 - 5 * 2 ;
    accept "7"            - 5 * 2 ;
    return(7)            - 5 * 2 ;
   return(7)             - 5 * 2 ;
  accept "-"             5 * 2 ;
 call parse_product      5 * 2 ;
  call parse_primitive   5 * 2 ;
   accept "5"            * 2 ;
   return(5)             * 2 ;
```

```
        accept "*"              2 ;
      call parse_primitive      2 ;
       accept "2"                 ;
        return(2)                 ;
      return(5*2 = 10)            ;
   return(7-10 = -3)              ;
 return(-3)                       ;
```

It should be clear from this trace why such a parser is called *recursive descent*. In particular, if a left parenthesis is encountered, it recursively parses a whole nested sub-expression (Figure 3.3).

More common uses for LL(1) parsing are to permit data files of flexible structure for everything from configuration data to application-specific problem-oriented languages. If used to input a POL, the parsing routines can be decorated with useful code, just as this example decorated them with calculation code. They can generate assembly language instructions to form a compiler. They can generate code for a higher-level language. They can build data structure. They can simply form an interpreter by performing intended actions as they read keywords. It doesn't take more than a dozen or so parsing subroutines to implement a fairly extensive language.

From the trace above it could seem that performance might be an issue. This is a matter of perception, resulting from the trickiness of the recursive control flow. Each subroutine call only takes on the order of ten instructions, counting argument passing, entry, and return, and in the trace above there are only *eleven* subroutine calls. By far the most instructions are spent inside *accept_token* as it gets characters, especially if there is a lot of whitespace and commentary. This is not to say that the parser couldn't be loaded down with inefficient decoration code.

It is worth pointing out the relationship between LL(1) parsing and problem-oriented languages.

- LL(1) is an easy way to implement a problem-oriented language, as the parser above implements a POL whose vocabulary is numbers, operation signs, and parentheses, and whose meaning is arithmetic calculation. (It's a POL because it's application-specific and it's non-redundant.)
- LL(1) is itself a POL. The vocabulary is *lexan()*, *token*, *token_long*, etc., which

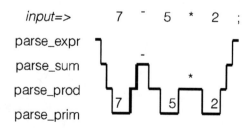

Figure 3.3. Parsing. Each subroutine accepts only tokens that make sense to it.

together with the base language C forms a POL for implementing languages. (If you want to alter the language that it parses, your edit count is low.) Note that the implementation of *this* language only required extending the base language C with some variables and functions. It didn't require its *own* parser.

In addition, in the calculator program above, there is an absolute minimum of application data structure, namely just a few local variables named "temp" and "op," along with pointers to them passed as arguments. This not only keeps the source code short and easy on run-time memory, but it avoids all the development cost of data structure, such as high edit count for modification, and deallocation bugs (freeing structures too soon or forgetting to free them). Students of compiler design might be inclined to ask, "Where's the parse tree? Don't you have to build a parse tree?" The parse tree is *implicit*. The only use for the parse tree is to walk it in suffix order so as to calculate the result. Since the execution trace of the parser is already a complete depth-first walk of the parse tree, it doesn't need its own storage to guide that walk. The information content of the parse tree is completely encoded by the input string itself and needs no other representation. On the other hand, if the problem requires that the input string be completely scanned at one time, and that the parse tree be walked (possibly in funny orders) at later times, then a physical parse tree or equivalent encoding (such as a string in Polish notation) is indicated.

DIFFERENTIAL PARSING

This section presents a partial solution to an important problem. In it, I try to combine the concepts of parsing and differential execution.

When any program reads input and generates output, the output is then redundant with the input. If either the input or the output information is subsequently altered, the two sets of information are no longer consistent and may need to be reconciled.

A good general example of this is a parser/generator for a context-free language. When a parser reads an input string and generates a parse tree or some such structure, its output is redundant with the input. Similarly, given a parse tree, a generator program can create a corresponding surface language string. So, given a context-free grammar, both parser and generator programs can be written for maintaining a two-way correspondence between redundant forms of data, the string and the parse tree. The two forms of data are not fully redundant, because some information in the string, such as whitespace and comments, does not find its way into the tree. Similarly, there may be information in the parse tree that does not find its way into the generated string. Nevertheless, it is a common problem to have two such representations of the same thing, both of which can be modified, and the separate modifications need to be resolved.

One approach is to do the resolving of differences in one representation or the other. For example, the new string could be parsed, generating a new parse tree, which could be compared with the old parse tree. Or the new parse tree could be used to generate a new string, which could be compared with the old string, but there is a question of how to handle the whitespace and comments.

The way this is presently done in commercial computer-aided software engineering (CASE) software is to keep *maps* which are yet a third data structure indicating a mapping between the first two representations. Keeping the maps themselves up-to-date makes the problem even harder.

What I try to do here, given a simple context-free grammar, is to write a program having three modes: *PRINT, PARSE*, and *MERGE*. In *PRINT* mode the program generates from parse tree to surface string. In *PARSE* mode it parses from surface string to parse tree, and in *MERGE* mode it simultaneously checks the two against each other. When the program finds a difference it goes into either *PRINT* mode or *PARSE* mode to walk over the mismatching constituents. In this way, it can detect the differences which can be used to update either representation without losing information such as comments.

In addition to this functioning, I want the source code to look like a declarative grammar. In other words, I want to write a single routine for each grammar rule, and have the routine automatically function in the proper way depending on the mode. The reason for this is so that I can easily modify the grammar. So here goes:

```
1  /* pdiff1.h */
2  #undef  P_LONG
3  #define P_LONG(tk,v)\
4      else if (token==T_LONG && (tk)==T_LONG && (v)==token_long) same = 1;
5
6  #undef  P_ID
7  #define P_ID(tk,s)\
8      else if (token==T_ID && (tk)==T_ID && strcmp((s),tokstr)==0) same = 1;
9
10 #undef  P_TOK
11 #define P_TOK(tk,c)\
12     else if (token==(c) && (tk)==(c)) same = 1;
13
14 #undef  P_ELSE
15 #define P_ELSE(tk)\
16     else if ((tk)==0) same = 1;
17
18
```

```
1  /* pdiff2.h */
2  #undef  P_LONG
3  #define P_LONG(tk,v)\
4      else if (token==T_LONG){(tk)=T_LONG; (v)=token_long; lexan();}
5
6  #undef  P_ID
7  #define P_ID(tk,s)\
8      else if (token==T_ID){(tk)=T_ID; strcpy((s),tokstr); lexan();}
9
10
```

```
 1 /* pdiff3.h */
 2 #undef  P_LONG
 3 #define P_LONG(tk,v)\
 4     else if ((tk)==T_LONG){printf("%d",(v));}
 5
 6 #undef  P_ID
 7 #define P_ID(tk,s)\
 8     else if ((tk)==T_ID){printf("%s",(s));}
 9
10
```

These first three header files define macros that will be used in the main program given below. They represent part of the attempt to convert the source code below into a problem-oriented language.

```
 1 /* pdiff.c  demonstration of differential parsing */
 2
 3 #include <stdio.h>
 4 #include "..\lexan\lexan.h"
 5
 6 #define LP '('
 7 #define RP ')'
 8
 9 struct prim_struct {          /* parse tree struct for primary */
10     int tok;          /* T_LONG, T_ID */
11     int i;
12     char name[10];
13     };
14
15 struct unary_struct {          /* parse tree struct for unary op */
16     int op;          /* 0<prim>, '-'<unary>, left paren<sum> */
17     void *p;
18     };
19
20 struct prod_struct {          /* parse tree struct for mult or div */
21     int op;          /* '*' or '/' */
22     struct unary_struct *left;
23     struct prod_struct *right;
24     };
25
26 struct sum_struct { /* parse tree struct for plus or minus */
27     int op;          /* '+' or '-' */
28     struct prod_struct *left;
29     struct sum_struct *right;
30     };
31
32 /* the three mode values */
33 #define PRINT 1
34 #define PARSE 2
35 #define MERGE 3
36
37 #define P (*pp)
```

```
38
39  int err = 0;
40  #define E if (err) goto L999
41
42  /* PRIM: PARSE/GEN A PRIMARY (ID OR NUMBER) */
43  void prim(struct prim_struct *P, int mode){
44      int show = 0;
45      int mode0 = mode, mode1 = mode;
46      err = 0;
47      if (mode==PARSE)
48              P = (struct prim_struct *)calloc(1, sizeof(*P));
49      if (mode==MERGE){
50  #include "pdiff1.h"
51              int same = 0;
52              if (0);
53              P_LONG(P->tok, P->i)
54              P_ID(P->tok, P->name)
55              if (!same){
56                      mode0 = PRINT;
57                      mode1 = PARSE;
58                      show = 1;
59                      }
60              }
61      for (mode=mode0; mode<=mode1; mode++){
62              if (show) printf(mode==PRINT ? "[" : "<");
63              if (mode & PARSE){
64  #include "pdiff2.h"
65                      if (0);
66                      P_LONG(P->tok, P->i)
67                      P_ID(P->tok, P->name)
68                      else
69                              err = 1;
70                      }
71  #include "pdiff3.h"
72              if (0);
73              P_LONG(P->tok, P->i)
74              P_ID(P->tok, P->name)
75              if (show) printf(mode==PRINT ? "]" : ">");
76              }
77      L999:;
78      }
79
80  void sum(struct sum_struct *P, int mode);
81
82  /* UNARY: PARSE/GEN A UNARY EXPRESSION */
83  void unary(struct unary_struct *P, int mode){
84      int show = 0;
85      int mode0 = mode, mode1 = mode;
86      err = 0;
87      if (mode==PARSE)
88              P = (struct unary_struct *)calloc(1, sizeof(*P));
89      if (mode==MERGE){
90              int same = 0;
91  #include "pdiff1.h"
92              /* if op is the same then recur */
93              if (0);
94              P_TOK(P->op,LP)
95              P_TOK(P->op,'-')
```

```
96                 P_ELSE(P->op)
97                 /* else if op is changed or new */
98                 if (!same) {
99                         mode0 = PRINT;
100                        mode1 = PARSE;
101                        show = 1;
102                        }
103             }
104     for (mode=mode0; mode<=mode1; mode++){
105                    if (show) printf(mode==PRINT ? "[" : "<");
106             if (mode & PARSE){
107                     if (token==LP){
108                             P->op = LP;
109                             lexan();
110                             }
111                     else if (token=='-'){
112                             P->op = '-';
113                             lexan();
114                             }
115                     else
116                             P->op = 0;
117                     }
118             if (P->op==LP){
119                     printf("%c", LP);
120                     sum(&P->p, mode); E;
121                     printf("%c", RP);
122                     }
123             else if (P->op=='-'){
124                     printf("%c", '-');
125                     unary(&P->p, mode); E;
126                     }
127             else {
128                     prim(&P->p, mode); E;
129                     }
130             if (mode & PARSE){
131                     if (P->op==LP){
132                             if (token==RP) lexan();
133                             else err = 1;
134                             }
135                     }
136             if (show) printf(mode==PRINT ? "]" : ">");
137             }
138     L999:;
139     }
140
141 /* PROD: PARSE/GEN A PRODUCT EXPRESSION */
142 void prod(struct prod_struct *P, int mode){
143     int show = 0;
144     int mode0 = mode, mode1 = mode;
145     err = 0;
146     if (mode==PARSE)
147             P = (struct prod_struct *)calloc(1, sizeof(*P));
148     unary(&P->left, mode); E;
149     if (mode==MERGE){
150             int same = 0;
151             /* if op is the same then recur */
152             if (token=='*'){
153                     if (P->op==token) same = 1;
```

```
154                         }
155             else if (token=='/'){
156                     if (P->op==token) same = 1;
157                     }
158             else {
159                     if (P->op==0) same = 1;
160                     }
161             /* else if op is changed or new */
162             if (!same){
163                     mode0 = PRINT;
164                     mode1 = PARSE;
165                     show = 1;
166                     }
167             }
168     for (mode=mode0; mode<=mode1; mode++){
169             if ((mode & PRINT) && P->op);
170             else if ((mode & PARSE) && (token=='*' || token=='/'));
171             else continue;
172             if (show) printf(mode==PRINT ? "[" : "<");
173             if (mode & PARSE){
174                     P->op = token; lexan();
175                     }
176             printf("%c", P->op);
177             prod(&P->right, mode); E;
178             if (show) printf(mode==PRINT ? "]" : ">");
179             }
180     L999:;
181     }
182
183 /* SUM: PARSE/GEN A SUM EXPRESSION */
184 void sum(struct sum_struct *P, int mode){
185     int show = 0;
186     int mode0 = mode, mode1 = mode;
187     err = 0;
188     if (mode==PARSE)
189             P = (struct sum_struct *)calloc(1, sizeof(*P));
190     prod(&P->left, mode); E;
191     if (mode==MERGE){
192             int same = 0;
193             /* if op is the same then recur */
194             if (token=='+'){
195                     if (P->op==token) same = 1;
196                     }
197             else if (token=='-'){
198                     if (P->op==token) same = 1;
199                     }
200             else {
201                     if (P->op==0) same = 1;
202                     }
203             /* else if op is changed or new */
204             if (!same){
205                     mode0 = PRINT;
206                     mode1 = PARSE;
207                     show = 1;
208                     }
209             }
210     for (mode=mode0; mode<=mode1; mode++){
211             if ((mode & PRINT) && P->op);
```

```
212                else if ((mode & PARSE) && (token=='+' || token=='-'));
213                else continue;
214                if (show) printf(mode==PRINT ? "[" : "<");
215                if (mode & PARSE){
216                     P->op = token; lexan();
217                     }
218                printf("%c", P->op);
219                sum(&P->right, mode); E;
220                if (show) printf(mode==PRINT ? "]" : ">");
221                }
222     L999:;
223     }
224
225 /* LEX_GETC: LEXAN REQUIRES US TO PROVIDE THIS */
226 int lex_getc(){
227     int c;
228     c = getc(stdin);
229     return c;
230     }
231
232 /* TOP OF PARSE TREE */
233 struct sum_struct *ptop;
234
235 /* MAIN */
236 void main(){
237     err = 0;
238     init_lexan();
239     sum(&ptop, PARSE); E;    /* parse string 1 into tree 1 */
240     if (token==';'){
241             putchar('\n');
242             lexan();
243             }
244     sum(&ptop, MERGE); E;    /* compare string 2 and tree 1 */
245     L999:;                   /* printing the comparison */
246     }
247
248
```

The language to be parsed has a simple context-free grammar:

```
    <primary> ::=
                    <integer>
                    <identifier>

    <unary expr> ::=
                    <primary>
                    | - <unary expr>
                    | ( <sum expr> )

    <product expr> ::=
                    <unary expr> [ *|/ <product expr> ]

    <sum expr> ::=
                    <product expr> [ +|- <sum expr> ]
```

The parse tree structures for each of these non-terminal symbols of the grammar are given in lines 9–30. The routine to parse/generate a primary is *prim* given in lines 42–78. The routine follows a common pattern: (1) If it is running as a parser, it allocates a structure to represent it (lines 47–48); (2) If it is in MERGE mode, meaning it is comparing an input stream with an existing parse tree, it looks for either an integer or an identifier (lines 53–54). The macros P_LONG and P_ID have been defined in *pdiff1.h* in such a way that they generate all the code we need at this point. In particular, they both parse the next token and compare it to the current parse tree node. If there is agreement, they set variable *same* to TRUE. If there is a discrepancy (lines 55–59), control variables *mode0, mode1,* and *show* are set up to control the loop that follows.

The loop (lines 61–76) is trying to accomplish the following:

If the mode on entry is PARSE, it simply parses (and incidentally prints the parse tree node).

If the mode on entry is PRINT, it simply prints the parse tree node.

If the mode on entry is MERGE and there is no discrepancy, it just prints the parse tree node. However, if there is a discrepancy, it executes two times, once in PRINT mode to print the old parse tree, and once in PARSE to scan the actual input (printing all the while). If it does this, it also prints brackets around the printed stream to indicate the mismatch.

The net result is a merged stream of tokens, with < > around things present in the input string, and [ ] around things present in the parse tree.

This same scheme is followed for the remaining grammar rules: *unary* (lines 82–139), *prod* (lines 141–181), and *sum* (lines 183–223).

Lines 225–230 are routine *lex_getc* needed by the lexical analyzer.

The main program (lines 235–246) inputs two expressions separated by a semicolon (;). The first one is parsed into a tree structure. The second is compared with the first, and the merged stream of tokens is printed.

The reason I say this program is experimental is that it contains a lot of repetitive boilerplate code, such as lines 168–179. If the program were written in a true problem-oriented language, that would all be invisible. By using the macros P_LONG, P_ID, P_TOK, and P_ELSE, I was partially able to bury the boilerplate. The goal would be to get rid of all the boilerplate and leave behind code that was structurally similar to the context-free grammar.

CONCLUSION

What is a language? Certainly C, Lisp, etc., are languages, but they are only *base* languages. The nouns and verbs available for expression include those of the base language, plus all variables, routines, and macros defined on top of it. When its redundancy drops it gradually changes from a language for stating *solutions* into a language for stating *problems*. The solution, in the form of the language's implementation, becomes generic. I think this is how progress will *really* be made in "software reuse."

A corollary of a language being reduced in redundancy is that the role of explicit data structures is lessened. Data structures contribute heavily to N, the redundancy measure, because they must be defined, allocated, filled, deallocated, etc., resulting in many separate pieces of source code. There may be data structures being used at run time, and that is another issue. There is a productivity benefit when programmers don't have to write code to deal with them.

This effect can be seen in the examples given so far. In the CIM simulation example, the source code shrunk by a factor of four, largely because it was describing the problem, not the solution. A similar situation exists with the *difex* package. Once the package is in place, displays can be programmed without declaring any display-related data.

4

Data

THE REPRESENTATION SPECTRUM

Data is data, and programs are programs, right? Data just lies there, and programs operate on it, correct? Data represents information, and programs have instructions for taking action.

This is the prevailing model of software, which I call the *object-action* model. I believe this is a weak model, and it doesn't take us into the future. We need something better.

Object-oriented programming (OOP) is a related model, in which data and programs are combined into *objects* that communicate by means of *messages*. This a very useful idea, but it is still a case of thinking in terms of entities with memory existing at run time being operated on by program scripts. It is still within the object-action model. This model will not go away.

However, I think we need to re-examine an idea that everyone knows but few understand, namely that the same information can be seen as data at one time and as program at another. This is not like OOP, in which an object contains distinct separate sets of bits representing program and data. Rather this idea means looking at the *same* bits as either program or data. I repeat, this concept is not new. Every compiler, interpreter, linker, loader, or assembler ever written deals with data that also happens to be program. What is new is the *appreciation* of what it has to say about software. For example, when one is designing a *data structure* to represent some information, one is also designing a *language* to represent the same information (if the concept of language is suitably broadened).

It is easy to see that a program is a collection of data. The program text may simply be considered as a stream of bits in some representation.

It may not be so easy to see arbitrary data as a kind of program. It becomes a little easier if you realize that, in a sense, data *controls* the programs that read it the same way instructions control a computer or an interpreter. Those programs are the interpreters of the data.

If data is an instruction set, what kind of instruction set is it, for what kind of computer? There is a very simple way to classify computers/interpreters, according to how much temporary working storage they need:

Linear: computers with no working memory at all, other than a program counter. Such a computer is incapable of conditional branching (because it can't remember a condition code).
Finite-State: computers with only a finite block of random access memory. Such a computer is incapable of arbitrary subroutine invocation (because the stack could overflow).
Stack: computers with unlimited last-in-first-out (LIFO) storage, plus a finite block of random access memory. Such a computer is incapable of arbitrary problems requiring random access to a data heap, such as simulation of physical processes.
Parallel: computers with unrestricted memory of more-than-sufficient size.

Similarly, when programs interpret data, they require a certain amount of temporary working storage. Depending on the amount and type required, whether none, finite, stack, or heap, a program falls into one of the above categories.

In the same way, every programming language falls into one of the above categories. Simple machine-tool programming languages, designed for once-through execution, require no branching. Languages such as the older versions of FORTRAN and COBOL provided a finite amount of working storage and could not do arbitrary recursive subroutine calls. Languages such as Algol provided recursive subroutine calls plus finite global memory, but were unable to express programs that can be handled by the next category. Languages such as Modula II, LISP, and any language that provides an arbitrary heap, can express unrestricted algorithms, in particular the simulation of parallel processes.

The importance of this is that you can consider any data as an instruction set falling at one of these levels of power. That means you can write interpreters for the data in languages at that level of power, or you can translate it into another instruction set or language at that level of power, or higher. This gives you lots of alternative ways to represent the information.

Linear Languages

A *linear language* (my definition) is one in which the programs simply execute once through and then finish. For example, to machine an aircraft component from an aluminum block requires a once-through machining program (represented physically as a rather long paper tape). I mean to include in this category any data or program that is simply interpreted or processed in a straight-through manner, with no decision-making.

Finite-State Languages

A *finite-state language* is one whose interpreter requires no more than finite storage. For example, in the older FORTRAN and COBOL versions, every array had to be declared with a fixed size, and subroutines had only static storage, so they could not be recursive. (In order for this classification system to work, we cannot allow using heap storage or external storage such as tape or disk. If these are allowed, all the language classes become equal in a rather uninteresting way.)

Finite-state representations are the mainstay of commercial applications, which is why languages such as COBOL, SQL, and sometimes FORTRAN are adequate. Most programs require no more than a fixed-size working storage allocation. Those programs that require more are considered "very difficult."

Stack Languages

A *stack language* is one whose interpreter requires a pushdown stack in addition to finite storage. For example, any language permitting recursive subroutine calling belongs to this class, such as C, Pascal, Algol, and PL/1.

Some data, to be printed, requires the printing program to have a pushdown stack of state variables to keep track. For example, a program to expand a manufacturing bill of materials (BOM) in depth-first order requires a pushdown stack as it prints assemblies, sub-assemblies, and so on down to the ultimate nuts and bolts.

Parallel Languages

The *parallel languages* are those whose interpreters require unrestricted heap storage, or at least one FIFO queue, or at least two LIFO stacks. Typically, these languages support lightweight processes, such as Modula II or Ada. This class also includes the object-oriented programming (OOP) languages, such as Smalltalk, Lisp with closures, Objective C, and C++. Some data, for example a manufacturing schedule, if printed out as a timeline, requires the printing program to maintain random access to a non-fixed set of state variables, one to track each concurrent activity. This makes it a parallel class language.

This language classification derives from a paper by Hewitt and Patterson [Hewitt 70], and it parallels the Automata Theory categories [Minsky 67] (finite state machines, pushdown automata, and Turing machines). It also parallels the Chomsky grammar classification (regular, context-free, context-sensitive).

In practical terms, these categories are not so firm. For example, one can use COBOL to write a bill-of-materials expansion program (depth-first) simply by using an array as the stack (Figure 4.1). The array, however, would have to be declared a finite size of n levels, for example, ten, so it could not handle a BOM of $n + 1$ levels, while in C, the language itself doesn't force one to put a limit on the stack size. The practical significance is that in COBOL the program is harder to

FINITE-STATE Language: STACK Language: SPECIFICATION:

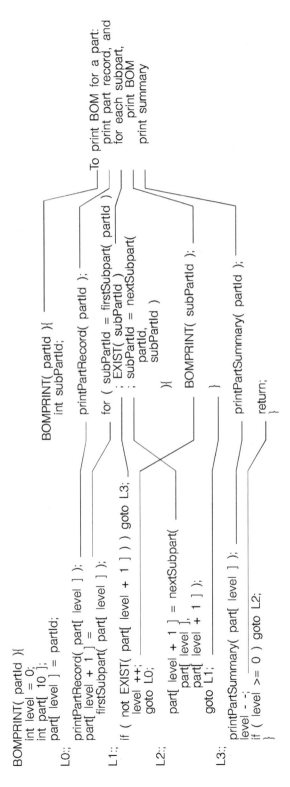

```
BOMPRINT( partId ){
  int level = 0;
  int part[ 10 ];
  part[ level ] = partId;
L0:;
  printPartRecord( part[ level ] );
  part[ level + 1 ] =
    firstSubpart( part[ level ] );
L1:;
  if ( not EXIST( part[ level + 1 ] ) ) goto L3;
    level ++;
    goto L0;
L2:;
    part[ level + 1 ] = nextSubpart(
      part[ level ],
      part[ level + 1 ] );
    goto L1;
L3:;
  printPartSummary( part[ level ] );
  level - -;
  if ( level >= 0 ) goto L2;
}
```

```
BOMPRINT( partId ){
  int subPartId;
  printPartRecord( partId );
  for ( subPartId = firstSubpart( partId )
    ; EXIST( subPartId )
    ; subPartId = nextSubpart(
        partId,
        subPartId )
    ){
    BOMPRINT( subPartId );
  }
  printPartSummary( partId );
  return;
}
```

```
To print BOM for a part:
  print part record, and
  for each subpart, print BOM
  print summary
```

Figure 4.1. Implementing a Bill Of Materials printing routine (depth first). The version on the left uses C as a finite state language (in which recursion is not permitted). The version on the right uses C as a stack language (in which recursion is permitted). The version on the right more closely resembles the specification. Because the problem requires stack memory, the stack must be simulated in the program on the left, with the result that the program is less maintainable. The lines show the correspondence between the parts of the two programs.

write than in C because in C the stack doesn't have to be implemented. It's already there, built into the language's control structure. It doesn't even have to be declared! Of course, it does require that the programmer know how and when to apply the powerful recursive programming technique. If the problem is changed slightly, to print the BOM in *breadth-first* order (that is, layer by layer), it is elevated to the parallel class (Figure 4.2). The print program must have a FIFO queue or something equivalent. If it is possible to encode the print program in a language having an implicit queue (e.g., parallelism primitives) the program can be simplified because the queue does not have to be simulated:

The reason for being aware of these categories is that, when a set of information is classified this way, it can be represented in any data structure or language in

FINITE STATE or STACK Language: **PARALLEL Language:**

```
#define QSIZ 256
int que[ QSIZ ];
unsigned int enq = 0, deq = 0;
int ninq = 0;
#define ENQUE(v) ( ninq++, enq++, \
    enq %= QSIZ, que[ enq ] = (v) )
#define DEQUE(v) ( ninq- -, deq++, \
    deq %= QSIZ, (v) = que[ deq ] )
#define QUE_NOT_EMPTY (ninq > 0)

BOMPART( partId ){
    int subPartId;
    ENQUE( partId );
    while( QUE_NOT_EMPTY ){
        DEQUE( partId );
        for ( subPartId = firstSubPart( partId )
            ; EXIST( subPartId )
            ; subPartId = nextSubPart(
                partId, subPartId )
            ){
            printPartRecord( subPartId );
            ENQUE( subPartId );
            }
        }
    }
```

```
BOM1( partId ){
    int subPartId ;
    printPartRecord( partId ) ;
    for ( subPartId = firstSubPart( partId ) ;
        ; EXIST( subPartId )
        ; subPartId = nextSubPart(
            partId,
            subPartId )
        ){
        printPartRecord( subPartId ) ;
        SPAWN( BOM1, subPartId ) ;
        }
}

BOMPART( partId ){
    SPAWN( BOM1, partId ) ;
    while ( RESUME() );
}
```

Figure 4.2. Implementing a Bill Of Materials printing routine (breadth first). The version on the left uses C as a less-than-parallel language that does not have a built-in queue. Thus, the queue has to be simulated, which makes the program less maintainable and which puts a finite limit on the queue's size. The version on the right assumes a parallel-level language that has a built-in queue of "big enough" size, in which program-argument pairs (objects) can be stored. The RESUME operation dequeues a program and argument, and calls the program with the argument. This is done, not to achieve process overlap, but to cause printing to occur in breadth-first order.

its category or higher. These implementation options can be arrayed and selected based on their pros and cons. The categories are summarized in Figure 4.3.

More About the Parallel Level

It may not be immediately obvious that languages at the parallel schematic level can be inter-translated. For example, why is it that a single FIFO queue is equivalent to an entire unrestricted heap, and that is equivalent to two LIFO stacks?

The *academic* reason is that there are multiple bases for computation. Without going into automata theory, computers can have different kinds of memory and

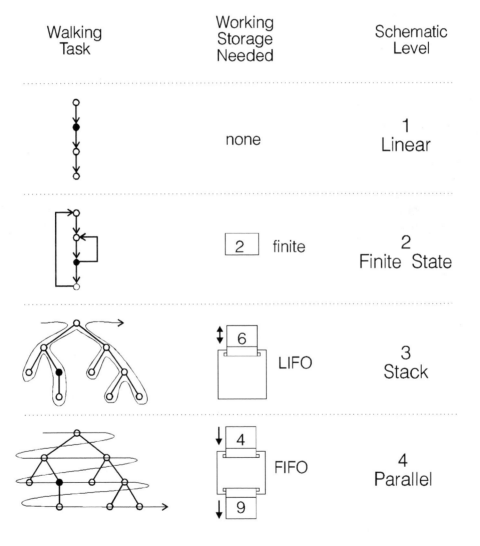

Figure 4.3. The working storage needed to accomplish a task determines its schematic level.

still be equivalent. One of them, a Turing Machine, has nothing but a two-way read-write tape. Another has two stacks, nothing more. Another has only a single FIFO queue. (You can think of a FIFO as random access memory because you can get to anything by circulating the contents of the FIFO.) These different kinds of computers are all equal in the sense that there is no program for one that can't be translated onto another.

The *practical* reason is that you can translate any program in any language into any language that supports either parallel processes or objects allocated from a heap. This is the most general category of language. However, there are programs written in C++ that cannot be translated down into Algol, a stack-level language. One such program is a program to do breadth-first tree walks (visiting each node only once), because to do that you need a FIFO of unbounded size. Similarly, there are programs in Algol that cannot be translated down into FORTRAN or COBOL, such as any program that requires unbounded recursion.

EXAMPLE: A DATABASE BRIDGE PROGRAM

In this example, what was thought to be data was better viewed as a program, and translating the data into C was the right solution.

A company was converting a large manufacturing database from hierarchical form to relational. The hierarchical database had become very complex over the years, with many fields intricately coded. Part of the conversion process was to "bridge" the two databases by a special program that could take segments from the hierarchical database and generate equivalent SQL statements. This is the type of nitty-gritty problem the real world has to solve daily (Figure 4.4). A central part of the bridge program was a "translation table," a table with thousands of rows that described the detailed layout of the fields in the hierarchical database, and what tables and columns they would map to in the relational database. When ordered by record ID, item ID, field offset, etc., the translation table itself had a hierarchical structure:

```
record-type
|   segment type
|   |   item type
|   |   |   word offset
|   |   |   | bit offset
|   |   |   | | bit size
|   |   |   | | | type of data
|   |   |   | | | |           destination table
|   |   |   | | | |           |           destination column
|   |   |   | | | |           |           | nulls allowed
|   |   |   | | | |           |           | |   special handling
|   |   |   | | | |           |           | |   |
P 016 005 11 4 28 N order_hist related_pn 1      ...
P 016 005 13 8  4 N order_hist cost_code  1 017 ...
P 016 005 14 0 24 N order_hist quantity   1      ...
```

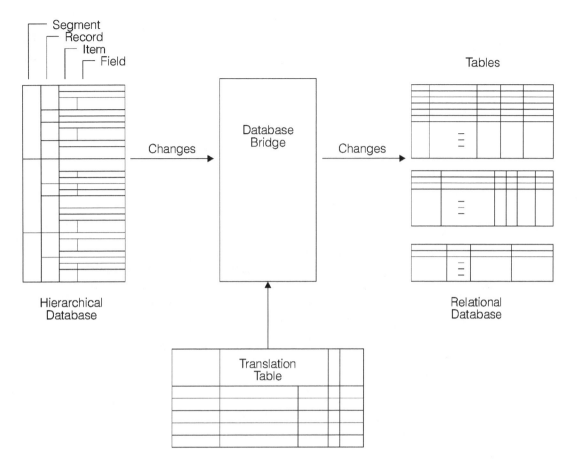

Figure 4.4. A database bridge problem. The old hierarchical database (left) and the new relational database (right) are in simultaneous use. Updates must travel from left to right. The bridge program is driven by a translation table that describes the mapping between the two databases.

A state-of-the-art software design was drawn up, complete with data flow diagrams and 1½-inch-thick design document. It was projected to take two man-years to implement, not including overruns. There were many unknowns, particularly concerning performance and memory load. The design was essentially a single program that would load the translation table into linked-list data structures. Then it would iterate through the hierarchical segment records, under the guidance of the loaded translation table, and generate SQL operations.

There is something out of balance about this design. Since performance is projected to be an issue, performance tuning comes into play. When the program runs, it looks at a data record, finds that record type in the translation table, looks for each field, finds that field in the translation table, dispatches on the type of translation, and generates the translation. There is a great deal of decision-making (information acquisition) going on. The next time a record of the same type is encountered, all that decision-making is repeated. The information gained previously has not been saved. Since the information in the translation table changes only on a weekly basis, this process is very wasteful in information-processing terms.

In such a case, precompiling should be considered. A precompiler would take the data that changes only very slowly, the translation table, and transform it into a generated program that does the same thing the original program would have done, but that doesn't have to waste time figuring out what to do (Figure 4.5).

This approach was taken and the job was completed by two people in less than three months, *four times faster* than the original estimate. The source code was about 0.5 inch thick, *three times smaller* than the *design* for the original program.

It is easy to see why the precompiling approach leads to good run-time performance, but it may not be obvious why it was so much easier to develop. I think it was a case of divide-and-conquer. The original program (let's call it the *interpreter*) had to deal with two different types of data structures simultaneously, the translation table and the run-time data. The precompiler had only one to deal with, the translation table. Furthermore, what the precompiler had to do with it was a

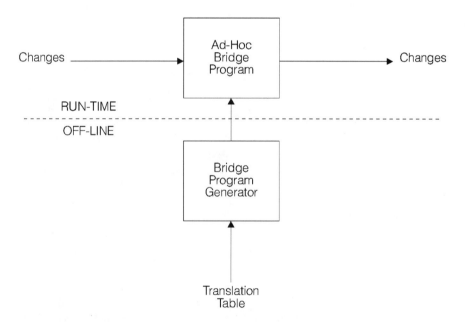

Figure 4.5. A simple implementation of the bridge. Because the translation table changes with low frequency, it is possible to translate the table into an ad hoc bridge program that operates at high speed. The program generator is a simpler program because it only has to deal with one input source.

straightforward transcription directly into a C program of similar hierarchical structure. Since its input was hierarchical, and its output was hierarchical, its data structure was principally a stack-like symbol table. It was not necessary to load the whole translation table into memory data structures, as in the original design.

Is the translation table data, or is it a program? Certainly it was data to begin with. It turned into a program when it was precompiled. It is easy to see that the translation table is like a statement in a language if you consider that an equivalent way to represent it would have been to use a simple LL(1) parsed character stream:

```
begin
   record type P
      segment type 016
         item type 005
            field 11 4 28 N order_hist.related_pn 1
            field 13 8  4 N order_hist.cost_code  1
            field 14 0 24 N order_hist.quantity   1
         item type ...
            ...
      segment type ...
         ...
      ...
   ...
end
```

If it is represented in this way, it makes a better database than its original form. The translation table is highly redundant (non-normalized) simply because every field has to say what record type, segment type, and item type it belongs to. This information is far more concise in the parsed string representation, and is therefore much easier to modify (with a text editor). It is true that it may be easier to get *reports* out of the relational table, but that was never part of the problem.

The bottom line is that seeing data as program can be a big win.

It is worth pointing out that there is no current published software engineering methodology that can recommend the construction of a precompiler. All methodologies (that I am aware of), including the object-oriented ones, are firmly based on the object-action model which sees a firm distinction between data and program.

SIMPLE OOP

Object-oriented programming first arose in the context of discrete simulation programs, such as simulations of telephone calls being routed through a phone system. In such a system there can be a variety of different types of objects in various stages of progress through the system. It is helpful if these objects can be very self-contained in the sense that adding a new type of object should not require major changes to the overall program.

The way this is done is, instead of having normal data records or structures that everyone has to know the definition of, each record is either marked with its type or contains a pointer to a procedure that knows how to do all actions that are peculiar to that type of record. The rest of the program communicates with these *objects* via standard interfaces, so that their internal details need not be known.

This idea has become wildly popular for a number of reasons, and it is a good idea. Problems that require independent active memory-holding entities, of which new types may easily arise, can hardly be solved *without* using OOP, if the term *OOP* is considered broadly enough. Such problems arise in discrete simulation, and they arise especially in reactive user interfaces.

Object-oriented programming can be done in any language. It is helpful to use C++ or Smalltalk or Lisp with closures, but you can also do it yourself without much difficulty.

The burning question with OOP is *should you use it?* I believe you should analyze the problem to see if you need it, and if so, use it. If not, don't. In either case, it is important to know how.

The basic idea is that in each application data record (in memory), there is a pointer to a function relating to that record. The pointer has to be at a standard offset in the record (like zero), so that callers do not have to care about the type of record. The function takes a variable number of arguments, at least two. The first argument is a pointer to the record, so that the function will know which instance of the record is being dealt with. The second is a message code telling the function what the caller would like done. Depending on the code, further arguments may or may not be needed.

For example, a simple video game could consist of several visible objects floating about in space, such as stars, planets, spaceships, etc. Here is a simple example of such a program:

```
1  /* oop.c  simple demonstration of object-oriented programming */
2
3  #include <stdio.h>
4  #include "..\fastmath\fastmath.h"
5  #include <graph.h>
6
7  enum msg_code {              /* message code definitions */
8      M_TICK,                  /* clock tick */
9      M_ACCELERATE,            /* accelerate an object */
10     M_PRINT,                 /* print an object */
11     M_SHOW,                  /* make object visible */
12     M_HIDE                   /* make object invisible */
13     };
14
15 extern int xorline(int x0, int y0, int x1, int y1, int color);
16
17 typedef int (*func_t)();
18
19 struct object {              /* the object superclass */
20     func_t func;
21     };
22
```

```
23                             /* the macro to send a message */
24 #define send(p,msg,a0,a1) ((*p->func)(p,msg,a0,a1))
25
26 #define WIDTH 640    /* EGA screen size */
27 #define HEIGHT 350
28
29 struct star {                     /* definition of star class */
30     func_t func;
31     FIXP x, y;
32     int visible;
33     char name[10];
34     };
35 void star_func(struct star *self, enum msg_code msg, FIXP a0, FIXP a1){
36     switch(msg){
37     break; case M_SHOW:;
38             if (!self->visible){
39                     xorline(TOLONG(self->x) - 10
40                             , TOLONG(self->y)
41                             , TOLONG(self->x) + 10
42                             , TOLONG(self->y)
43                             , 15);
44                     xorline(TOLONG(self->x)
45                             , TOLONG(self->y) - 10
46                             , TOLONG(self->x)
47                             , TOLONG(self->y) + 10
48                             , 15);
49                     self->visible ^= 1;
50                     }
51     break; case M_HIDE:;
52             if (self->visible){
53                     xorline(TOLONG(self->x) - 10
54                             , TOLONG(self->y)
55                             , TOLONG(self->x) + 10
56                             , TOLONG(self->y)
57                             , 15);
58                     xorline(TOLONG(self->x)
59                             , TOLONG(self->y) - 10
60                             , TOLONG(self->x)
61                             , TOLONG(self->y) + 10
62                             , 15);
63                     self->visible ^= 1;
64                     }
65     break; case M_PRINT:;
66             printf("Star %s at <%d, %d>\n"
67                     , self->name
68                     , (int)TOLONG(self->x)
69                     , (int)TOLONG(self->y)
70                     );
71         }
72     }
73 struct star * new_star(FIXP x, FIXP y, char *name){
74     struct star *p = (struct star*)malloc(sizeof(*p));
75     p->func = star_func;
76     p->x = x;
77     p->y = y;
78     p->visible = 0;
79     strcpy(p->name, name);
80     return(p);
```

```
 81      }
 82
 83  struct ship {                               /* definition of ship class */
 84      func_t func;
 85      FIXP x, y;
 86      FIXP vx, vy;
 87      int visible;
 88      int serial_num;
 89      };
 90  void ship_func(struct ship *self, enum msg_code msg, FIXP a0, FIXP a1){
 91      switch(msg){
 92      break; case M_SHOW:;
 93              if (!self->visible){
 94                      xorline(TOLONG(self->x)
 95                            , TOLONG(self->y)
 96                            , TOLONG(self->x) + 1
 97                            , TOLONG(self->y)
 98                            , 14);
 99                      self->visible ^= 1;
100                      }
101      break; case M_HIDE:;
102              if (self->visible){
103                      xorline(TOLONG(self->x)
104                            , TOLONG(self->y)
105                            , TOLONG(self->x) + 1
106                            , TOLONG(self->y)
107                            , 14);
108                      self->visible ^= 1;
109                      }
110      break; case M_TICK:;
111              send(self,M_HIDE,0,0);
112              self->x += self->vx;
113              self->y += self->vy;
114              send(self,M_SHOW,0,0);
115      break; case M_ACCELERATE:;
116              self->vx += a0;
117              self->vy += a1;
118      break; case M_PRINT:;
119              printf("Ship %d at <%d, %d>\n"
120                    , self->serial_num
121                    , (int)TOLONG(self->x)
122                    , (int)TOLONG(self->y)
123                    );
124          }
125      }
126  struct ship * new_ship(FIXP x, FIXP y, FIXP vx, FIXP vy, int serial_num){
127      struct ship *p = (struct ship*)malloc(sizeof(*p));
128      p->func = ship_func;
129      p->x = x;
130      p->y = y;
131      p->vx = vx;
132      p->vy = vy;
133      p->visible = 0;
134      p->serial_num = serial_num;
135      return(p);
136      }
137
138  void main(){
```

```
139     int n = 0;
140     struct star *st1 = new_star(
141             TOFIXP((long)WIDTH/2)
142           , TOFIXP((long)HEIGHT/2)
143           , "Altair"
144           );
145     struct ship *sh1 = new_ship(
146             TOFIXP((long)WIDTH/2-100)
147           , TOFIXP((long)HEIGHT/2)
148           , TOFIXP(0), TOFIXP(0)
149           , 87654
150           );
151
152     _setvideomode(_ERESCOLOR);     /* setup */
153     _clearscreen(_GCLEARSCREEN);
154     send(st1,M_SHOW,0,0);
155     send(sh1,M_SHOW,0,0);
156     while(1){
157             for (n=100; --n>0 && !kbhit(); );
158             if (kbhit()){
159                     int c = getch();
160                     if (c=='q') break;
161                     else if (c=='u')
162                             send(sh1, M_ACCELERATE
163                                   , TOFIXP(0), TOFIXP(-1)
164                                   );
165                     else if (c=='d')
166                             send(sh1, M_ACCELERATE
167                                   , TOFIXP(0), TOFIXP( 1)
168                                   );
169                     else if (c=='l')
170                             send(sh1, M_ACCELERATE
171                                   , TOFIXP(-1), TOFIXP(0)
172                                   );
173                     else if (c=='r')
174                             send(sh1, M_ACCELERATE
175                                   , TOFIXP( 1), TOFIXP(0)
176                                   );
177                     }
178             {
179                     long dx = TOLONG(sh1->x - st1->x);
180                     long dy = TOLONG(sh1->y - st1->y);
181                     long dx2 = dx * dx;
182                     long dy2 = dy * dy;
183                     long r2 = dx2 + dy2;
184                     long r;
185                     for (r=0; r*r<r2; r++); /* square root */
186                     if (r2==0) r2 = 1;
187                     send(sh1, M_ACCELERATE
188                           , ((TOFIXP(-dx)/r)*50)/r2
189                           , ((TOFIXP(-dy)/r)*50)/r2
190                           );
191                     }
192             send(st1,M_TICK,0,0);
193             send(sh1,M_TICK,0,0);
194             }
195     _setvideomode(_DEFAULTMODE);   /* finish */
196     }
197
```

In this program there are two object classes, *star* and *ship*. The star object class is defined in lines 29–72, and a routine to create one is at line 73. Similarly the ship object class is defined in lines 83–136.

The main routine (line 138) simply makes a star and a ship, shows them on the screen, and enters a simulation loop.

Periodically, until the user types the letter *q* for quit, the objects are told that a clock TICK has gone by (lines 192–193), so they can move themselves on the screen.

If the user types a letter *u* for up, *d* for down, *r* for right, and *l* for left, the ship is given a kick of acceleration in the indicated direction (lines 161–176). In lines 178–191, there is some logic to make the ship accelerate toward the star, so that it moves in an orbit (somewhat inaccurately).

The common interface is represented by the macro *send* (line 24) which calls an object's function. The first argument is the object itself, the second is a message code (defined in lines 7–13), and the rest are arbitrary arguments. The message codes are M_TICK meaning a unit of time has passed, M_PRINT meaning to print oneself, M_ACCELERATE meaning to modify one's velocity, M_SHOW to make oneself visible on the screen, and M_HIDE to make oneself invisible. New classes of objects can be added to the program, and if they handle these messages they will be able to move around the screen.

The point of this is that objects become known by their behavior when responding to messages, not by the fields in their records. An *abstract data type* is just a set of message codes along with an understanding of what they mean. Any object that responds properly to those message codes is considered to belong to that abstract data type. (By the way, the piece of code that responds to a message is called a *method* or *virtual function*.)

A very common and useful abstract data type is the *stream*, which is a generalization of the idea of an open file. It responds at a minimum to messages M_READ and M_WRITE. One kind of stream object can actually do I/O to real files. As long as the application programs perform I/O by sending messages to stream objects, it is easy to make them talk to new types of streams that didn't exist before. For example, a graphical window object could be made to respond to stream messages. If told to write a string, it could print it for the user. If told to read, it could solicit keyboard input. Even little things, like data entry fields in a form, could be streams.

Another useful abstract data type is a *displayable_object*, which is anything that responds to messages M_SHOW to present it on a screen and M_ERASE to erase it. For example, the window objects mentioned above would respond to these messages, at a minimum. When a type of object responds to the messages of an abstract data type, it is said to *inherit from* that data type. For example, a window object could inherit from both the stream and displayable_object abstract data types.

The danger in OOP is to feel that if you're not defining object classes you're not doing object-oriented programming. But objects are fundamentally data, and much of this book is about how data should be minimized. I think the way to tell when OOP is being well-used is when very few classes need to be defined and the overall application code is very concise.

CO-ROUTINES, STATE MACHINES, FLYWEIGHT PROCESSES

Lightweight processes are a feature of the OS/2 operating system, as well as languages like Modula II and Ada. The idea is to have multiple threads of control within a single address space, explicitly sharing data. These processes are called *lightweight* because they don't require much of the overhead of heavy processes, such as paging tables, IO device allocations, interrupt vectors, and so on. Sometimes this is done for performance reasons, to exploit parallel CPU hardware. However, it is probably more useful as a way of structuring code, regardless of the hardware. In particular, programs that must wait on and process input through multiple asynchronous input streams are often best written as closely coupled parallel processes.

In this technique, we notice that real-time control programs in particular often have to keep track of a large number of external objects whose states may have to change asynchronously. Often the states of those external objects are constrained to change in a predictable pattern according to some finite state machine. For each external object there is a data record in memory maintaining its state. We can turn that data record into a *flyweight process* by letting its finite state machine take the form of a real subroutine, and let its state variable decide where it resumes control in that subroutine. This both simplifies the code and simplifies the process of making changes to the state machine. It enhances performance by simplifying access to data related to the object. It also enhances reliability by reducing opportunity for errors, particularly in regard to memory allocation and freeing.

The basic idea is that the external object is modeled by a structure that, in addition to normal variables, contains a state variable having values like 0, 1, and 2, and a pointer to an executable function:

```
struct object_struct {
        int state;
        int (*func)();
     .. other object-related vars ..
        }
```

The function pointed to is shown below. Its only argument is a pointer to the process object. The very first line of code in the function is a macro DISPATCH*n* (given below) where *n* is the number of states in the state machine. This macro contains code to test the state and jump to the proper place in the code. If the state is 0, it just falls into the first statements after the DISPATCH. If the state is 1, it jumps to the statement following STATE(1,L1), and so on. After the final logic, the function kills itself by freeing its memory.

```
object_func(p) struct object_struct *p;{
        DISPATCH2;
     .. application-specific logic ..
```

```
    .. STATE(1,L1);
    .. .. application-specific logic ..
    .. STATE(2,L2);
    .. .. application-specific logic ..
    .. free(p);
    .. }

#define DISPATCH2\
    .. if (state==1) goto L1;\
    .. if (state==2) goto L2;
```

To make an object of this type, a function like the following is called. It allocates storage for the object, initializes its state and function pointer and any other variables that need initializing. Then it gives the brand-new process an initial shot of time by RESUME-ing it. Control comes back as soon as the object's state machine function does a STATE.

```
spawn_object(.. initial value arguments ..){
    .. struct object_struct *p;
    .. *p = malloc(sizeof(*p));
    .. p->state = 0;
    .. p->func = object_func;
    .. .. init other vars p->..
    .. RESUME(p);
    .. }
```

The RESUME operation consists of calling the object's state machine function (Figure 4.6), passing the pointer to the object itself as the only argument:

```
#define RESUME(p) ((*p->func)(p))
```

The WAIT operation gives up control for a small amount of time, to allow other flyweight processes a chance to run (Figure 4.7). It takes two arguments, a state number and a state label. It sets the object's state, puts a pointer to the object in a wait queue, and gives up control. Later when the object is resumed, control will come back to the state label and fall through. Because C language, like assembly language, allows jumping to labels anywhere within a function, WAITs can be placed inside of loops or conditionals without any problem.

```
#define WAIT(st,lab)\
    .. p->state = st;\
    .. ENQUE(p);\
    .. return;\
    .. lab:;
```

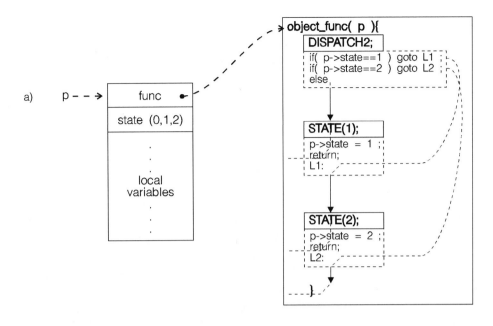

Figure 4.6. A flyweight process is a data record (a) containing a function pointer and an integer state variable. The RESUME operation (b) causes the flyweight process to continue executing from its previous STATE statement, and proceed to the next STATE statement that it encounters. (Normally, the final state is placed inside an infinite WHILE loop so that the flyweight process never actually reaches the end. Alternatively, the record simply can be deleted at the appropriate time.)

Overall control consists of spawning lightweight processes and running them. This top level program creates three flyweight processes and then enters a dispatch loop, resuming processes in a round-robin fashion until none are left alive.

```
toplevel(){
    .. spawn_object(.. optional args ..);
    .. spawn_object(.. optional args ..);
    .. spawn_object(.. optional args ..);
    .. while(ninq){
            struct object_struct *p;
            sleep(1);/* wait 1 second, if desired */
            DEQUE(p);
            RESUME(p);
            }
    }
```

```
while ( ... ) {
    STATE( 3 ) ;

    if ( ... ) {
        for ( p->i = 0; p->i < p->n; p->i ++ ){
            STATE( 4 ) ;
        }
    }
}
```

Figure 4.7. States can be placed inside of arbitrarily nested conditional, looping, or other compound statements. For example, to wait for some external condition to be satisfied, simply code a wait loop with a state inside it. All local variables of the state machine, such as loop counters, and so forth, are based on pointer p, because they are located in the state machine record.

Finally, the wait queue itself is rather straightforward. It consists of an array of pointers to objects. There are two index variables, one for *enque*, and one for *deque*, that advance circularly around the array. A third variable keeps track of how many pointers are in the queue, so as to check for when it is empty.

```
#define QUESIZ 256
unsigned int enq=0, deq=0, ninq=0;
struct object_struct *que[QUESIZ];

#define EMPTY (ninq==0)
#define ENQUE(p)\
        (que[enq++]=(p), enq%=QUESIZ, ninq++)
#define DEQUE(p)\
        ((p)=que[deq++], deq%=QUESIZ, ninq-)
```

How does it all work? The top-level routine spawns the first object. It executes as far as its first WAIT statement, at which point it puts itself in the queue and returns to the top level. The top level then spawns the second object, which does the same thing. After spawning the third object, all three objects are in the queue. Then, the loop is entered. A pointer to an object is removed from the queue and the object is RESUMED. When the object gets to its second WAIT statement, it puts itself back in the queue and returns, at which time the next pointer is removed from the queue, and so on. This goes on in a round-robin fashion. When some object is resumed in its final state, the object performs its final statements, frees its own memory, and returns without replacing itself in the queue. This is how processes die. When the processes are all dead, the queue is empty, and the top level loop stops (Figure 4.8).

a)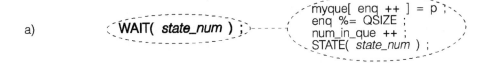

b)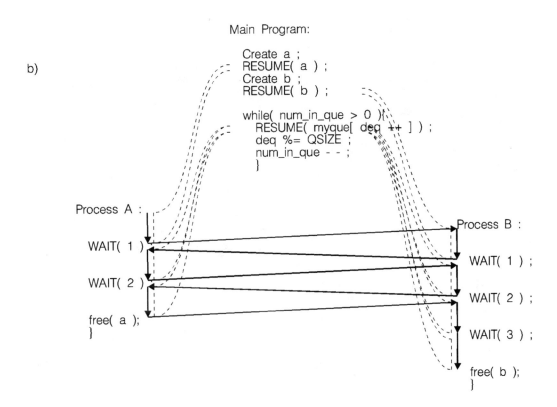

Figure 4.8. Parallel execution of flyweight processes. A WAIT state (a) is a state during which a pointer to the process resides in a FIFO run queue. Execution (b) requires a main program that creates the initial processes, resumes them, and then runs a dispatch loop in which processes are removed from the queue and resumed. Execution ceases when the queue becomes empty. The perceived flow of control is indicated by solid lines, and the actual flow of control is shown by dashed lines. A flyweight process terminates by returning without placing itself back in the queue. It can also release its storage at that time. States need not be encountered in sequential order.

In using flyweight processes, one quickly runs into the need to have subroutines with states inside them. To accomplish this, we need the new macros CALL and RETURN. CALL spawns a subordinate process and waits for it to complete. RETURN terminates a subordinate process and resumes its caller. The only new data needed to implement this is a caller pointer in each state machine record. If a state machine has not been CALLed from another state machine, its caller pointer is NULL (Figure 4.9).

To complete the big picture, it is important to understand how flyweight processes should be used. They should be used as a replacement for state machines coded the old way. They should not be used unless you would otherwise have to use state machines coded the old way. And they should not be used as a substitute for system-level processes or threads.

For example, in the simulation program given in Appendix C, a flyweight process is spawned to represent each requested manufacturing job. This is because we

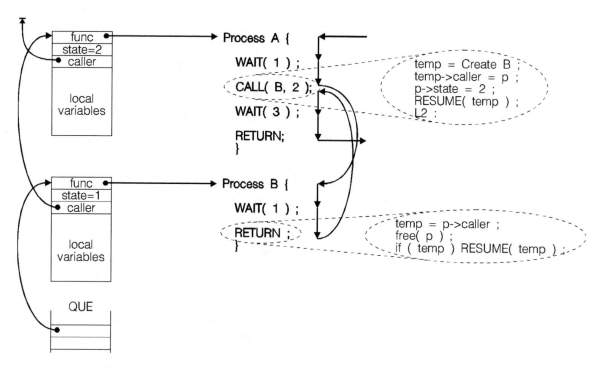

Figure 4.9. Flyweight process A calling flyweight process B as a subroutine. Each process record has a pointer to its calling process (or NULL). The CALL statement creates the subprocess record, sets its caller, and resumes it. The RETURN statement deletes the subprocess's record and resumes the caller, if there is one. (Process A has a NULL caller because it has not been CALLed from another process.) In this example, process B is waiting in the queue. The accessibility of the records is from the queue through the chain of caller pointers.

would otherwise have to represent each job by a record having a complex set of states. Now, we don't have a record *and* a flyweight process; the record *is* the flyweight process, and the flyweight process *is* the record. (This minimizes data redundancy.) The only difference is that the source code that takes actions is now organized in a way that makes sense, whereas before it would have been scattered about in event handlers.

Because a manufacturing job must go through many common sub-sequences, flyweight process subroutines are used. At any given time, there may be dozens of flyweight processes, deep inside subroutines, time-sharing the overall process (Figure 4.10).

GARBAGE COLLECTION

Much of this book is about how to avoid redundancy. A principal way to avoid redundancy is to avoid data structure. However, if you must use data structure, you can at least try to minimize the kinds of headaches it can cause for you.

In these days of C++, a popular term for one of these problems is in the air: *memory leak*. When a program fails to free all the memory blocks that it allocates

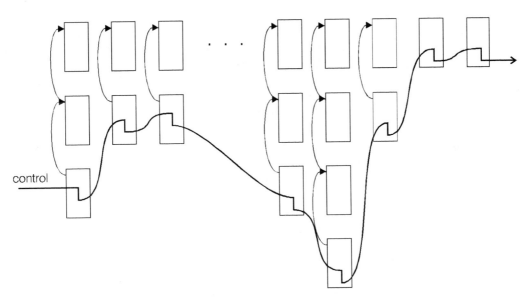

Figure 4.10. Many flyweight processes can be active at the same time, limited only by storage and queue size. Flyweight processes are best used to keep track of individual application objects following a sequenced script of some kind, such as a manufacturing job or a client/server request. They are applicable when the alternative is the use of state machine records and/or event-driven processing.

from the heap, it is said to *leak memory*. After a while, such a program's memory pool dries up. There is technology being developed to sniff out and track down memory leaks and related bugs.

It takes a great deal of programmer discipline to avoid memory leaks. It also helps to have a simple hierarchical data structure, without having more than one pointer to any memory block. This makes it easier to keep track of who *owns* it. This has the effect of limiting what can be done, because programmer time that could be spent on functionality is instead spent on memory discipline.

The approach of using a *garbage collector* has a lot to recommend it. If the total amount of memory to be managed is not very large, it is quite fast. It leads to very robust software because there are fewer ways to have memory bugs, and the bugs that can occur are more benign, compared to the do-it-yourself discipline approach.

Some languages have built-in garbage collectors, notably Lisp and Smalltalk. It is important to understand what a garbage collector is and why it is useful. Recall that problems requiring flexible use of heap storage are at the parallel schematic level in the language hierarchy. Experimental artificial intelligence (AI) programs tend to be at this level. Programs that make extensive use of heap storage (that is, the function *malloc()* in C) have a common problem, namely deciding when objects should be released back to the heap.

If an object is currently pointed at by a global pointer variable, it is *accessible*. If it is pointed at by a local pointer variable in a currently active function, it is also accessible. If it is pointed at by a pointer in another accessible data object, then it is accessible. Otherwise it is *inaccessible*, and the application program will never see it again. When that is the case, it should be released back to the heap and not before. This is an *invariant condition*. When complex data structures are being built and modified, that use many shared components, any given object may be accessible via multiple pointers, and in general, it may be very difficult for any given piece of source code to know for sure when it is safe to free something.

There are two kinds of insidious bugs that occur when programs attempt to decide when to free things. The first bug occurs when the program frees something while it is still accessible. This has the result that the storage may be subsequently allocated for another purpose and filled with data, while it is still being used for the first purpose. This bug is hard to find, because the corrupted data may not be discovered for some time, there is no clue as to where the corrupting data is coming from, and the source of corrupting data is not the part of the program that is at fault. The second bug occurs when the program fails to free something as it becomes inaccessible. (It can't be freed *after* it becomes so!) The symptom of this bug is unexplained exhaustion of heap storage. The symptom occurs long after the faulty program committed the bug, so it is hard to find. In fact, the less often the bug occurs, the more time will pass before the symptom becomes noticeable.

These bugs are common in large programs written in C, Pascal, PL/1, or FORTRAN when they build large linked-list data structures, and in my experience they account for a good fraction of development time.

One often-tried solution to this problem is called the *reference-count* method. Each block of storage, as it is allocated, contains a field that is a count of the pointers pointing at it. This is an *invariant condition*. To respect this invariant condition, pointer operations must be closely supervised. When a pointer is set to point to a block, the counter on that block must be incremented. When a pointer to a block is changed so it no longer points at it, the count must be decremented. If that causes the count to go to zero, the block is freed. This is not always easy to do. For example, if a pointer to a block is passed to a subroutine, that actually creates another pointer. If a subroutine has local pointer variables pointing at blocks, they must be carefully cleared before allowing the subroutine to return. Not only that, but care must be taken to attend to pointers *only* if they point at blocks in the heap, and only blocks which are being reference counted. Pointers elsewhere should not be handled this way. All of this adds up to a scheme which is difficult to make reliable in a language that does not provide it as a built-in capability.

Another approach to this problem is to use a less-flexible data structure. If the data structure is restricted to simple trees or linked lists, with no shared blocks, objects can be freed when their parent pointers are cleared. Still another approach is to avoid freeing things altogether. The data structure is built up, used, and when the heap becomes exhausted, the accessible data structure is printed out to a file and the program ends. Later, the program is started up again and the data is read from the file into a fresh heap. This last technique is the germ of a really good idea, the *copying garbage collector* [Baker 78].

In a copying garbage collector there are two heaps, the current one and the standby. Storage is allocated in a linear fashion out of the current heap. At some point in time before the current heap becomes exhausted, all of its accessible contents are copied to the standby, leaving the garbage behind. Then the current heap is declared to be empty and the two heaps reverse roles. It is nicely behaved because it compacts the storage and the time it takes is proportional to the amount of accessible storage, not the amount of garbage.

The copying of storage from one heap to the other is straightforward. Starting from a pointer to a block, the block is copied to the second heap. In the place where the block had been, a forwarding pointer is deposited, marked as such. Then the original pointer is modified to point to the new copy of the block, and the process is performed recursively on all pointers inside the block. When the process follows a pointer to a block and discovers that the block has already been copied (by finding a marked forwarding pointer there), it simply sets the pointer pointing to the copy. That is how shared structure is handled (Figure 4.11).

To start the process off, there needs to be a set of global pointers from which all accessible structure hangs. A few distinguished pointer variables or a short array is usually sufficient. Although objects can be pointed at by pointers in active subroutines, either the copying process can be delayed until they return to the top level, or the addresses of those pointer variables can be registered in a special array.

What kinds of bugs can occur? If a program fails to register a pointer to a data structure, the result is that the data structure is freed, reallocated, and used. Since any program using data structure probably examines it before modifying it, the program will discover that the data structure has been clobbered before it over-writes the new user's data. In this way, the malfunction is usually confined to the

Old Pool   Forwarding   New Pool
Pointers

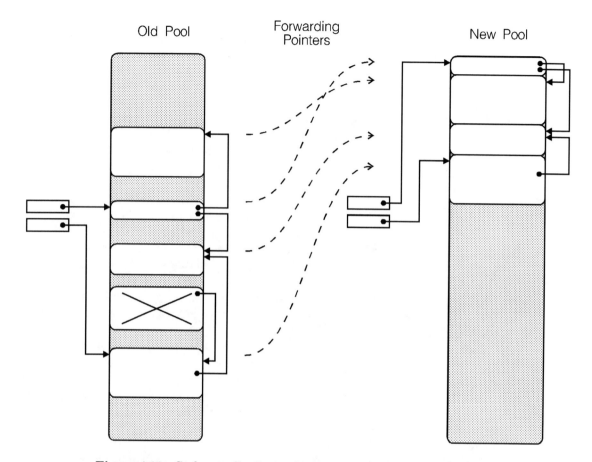

Figure 4.11. Garbage collection and compaction. The blocks accessible
from the external registers are packed together. The inaccessible blocks
(marked X) are returned to free storage.

code that caused it. On the other hand, registering a pointer unnecessarily causes
some data structure to be retained longer than necessary, but not in a steadily
growing amount.

Following is a simple garbage collector that can be adapted for any purpose:

```
1 /* gc.h   simple copying garbage collector */
2
3 #include "types.h"
4
5 #ifdef IN_GC
6 #define DEFVAR(typ,name) typ name
7 #else
8 #define DEFVAR(typ,name) extern typ name
9 #endif
10
```

```
11 DEFVAR(int,   gcHeapSize );
12 DEFVAR(int,   gcWhichHeap);
13 DEFVAR(char*, gcHeap[2]  );
14 DEFVAR(int,   gcUsed     );
15
16 /* use P as if it were a "by reference" argument named P */
17 #define P (*pp)
18
19 BOOL GcOpen(int size);
20 void GcClose();
21 void * GcMalloc(int size);
22 int GcFreeSpace();
23 void GcSwapHeaps();
24 BOOL GcCopyForward(void *P, int size);
25
26 #undef DEFVAR
27
```

This header file defines the two heaps. The heap currently being used for allocation, *gcHeap[0]* or *[1]*, is selected by *gcWhichHeap*. Allocation in the current heap is done linearly. Variable *gcUsed* tells how much of the current heap has been allocated and determines where the next allocation will take place.

```
 1 /* gc.c  simple copying garbage collector */
 2
 3 #define IN_GC
 4 #include "gc.h"
 5
 6 /* macro to round an integer up to a multiple of 4 */
 7 #define ROUNDUP4(n)(((n) + 3) & ~3)
 8
 9 /* macro to free a block of memory */
10 #define FREE(p)((p)!=NULL ? (free(p), (p)=NULL) : NULL)
11
12 /* error-checking macro */
13 #define ASSERT(test) ((test) ? 0 : exit(1))
14
15 /* GcOpen(size): allocate two heaps of given size */
16 /*   return FALSE if error */
17
18 BOOL GcOpen(int size){
19     size = ROUNDUP4(size);
20     gcWhichHeap = 0;
21     gcHeap[0] = (char*)malloc(size);
22     if (gcHeap[0]==NULL) return FALSE;
23     gcHeap[1] = (char*)malloc(size);
24     if (gcHeap[1]==NULL){
25             FREE(gcHeap[0]);
26             return FALSE;
27             }
28     gcHeapSize = size;
29     }
```

```
30
31 /* GcClose(): clean up when finished */
32
33 void GcClose(){
34     FREE(gcHeap[0]);
35     FREE(gcHeap[1]);
36     gcHeapSize = gcWhichHeap = gcUsed = 0;
37     }
38
39 /* GcMalloc(size): allocate a block of given size from heap */
40
41 void * GcMalloc(int size){
42     void * p = gcHeap[gcWhichHeap] + gcUsed;
43     /* Round up to size of 4N */
44     size = ROUNDUP4(size);
45     /* If block won't fit, don't allocate it */
46     if (gcUsed + size > gcHeapSize)
47             return NULL;
48     /* Else allocate the block, clear and return it */
49     gcUsed += size;
50     memset(p, 0, size);
51     return p;
52     }
53
54 /* int GcFreeSpace(): return space remaining for allocation */
55
56 int GcFreeSpace(){
57     return gcHeapSize - gcUsed;
58     }
59
60 /* GcSwapHeaps(): call this at start of garbage collection */
61
62 void GcSwapHeaps(){
63     gcWhichHeap ^= 1;
64     gcUsed = 0;
65     }
66
67 /* BOOL GcCopyForward(pp, size): utility used by ad hoc copy routines
68    to copy blocks to next heap.
69    Returning TRUE means caller should also copy subordinate pointers.
70 */
71
72 BOOL GcCopyForward(void *P, int size){
73     /* Save address of old copy */
74     void **old = P;
75     /* If pointer is null, do nothing */
76     if (P==NULL) return FALSE;
77     /* If the block has already been moved,
78        modify the pointer and notify caller */
79     if ((long)(old[0]) & 1){
80             P = (void*)((long)(old[0]) & ~1);
81             return FALSE;
82             }
83     /* Otherwise */
84     /* Set pointer to a new copy */
85     P = GcMalloc(size);
86     /* If it doesn't fit, something is broken */
87     ASSERT(P != NULL);
```

```
88     /* Copy the contents into the new block */
89     memcpy(P, old, size);
90     /* Store the forwarding pointer */
91     old[0] = (void*)((long)P | 1);
92     /* Notify caller to chase the sub-pointers */
93     return TRUE;
94     }
```

This file contains the generic garbage collection routines. Routine *GcOpen(size)* (lines 15–29) initializes the heaps. *GcClose* cleans it up. Routine *GcMalloc(size)* does the job of *malloc()* in the C heap. *GcFreeSpace()* tells how much space is left in the current heap.

GcSwapHeaps() is used to start the process of garbage collection. All it does is switch heaps and restart allocation.

The workhorse of the garbage collector is *GcCopyForward* (lines 67–94). It will be used in a special way to copy a block of memory from the old heap to the new one and leave behind a forwarding pointer. Also it modifies the pointer to the block so that is points to the new block.

```
 1 /* gctest.c  test the GC routines */
 2
 3 #include <stdio.h>
 4
 5 #include "gc.h"
 6
 7 void copy_yyy(struct yyy *P);
 8
 9 struct xxx {
10     struct xxx * px;
11     struct yyy * py;
12     int data;
13     };
14
15 struct yyy {
16     struct yyy * py;
17     int data;
18     };
19
20 void copy_xxx(struct xxx *P){
21     if (GcCopyForward(&P, sizeof(*P))){
22             copy_xxx(&(P->px));
23             copy_yyy(&(P->py));
24             }
25     }
26
27 void copy_yyy(struct yyy *P){
28     if (GcCopyForward(&P, sizeof(*P))){
29             copy_yyy(&(P->py));
30             }
31     }
32
33 void main(){
```

```
34        struct xxx *px = NULL;
35        /* allocate heaps */
36        GcOpen(1024);
37        /* Create a tree structure */
38        px = GcMalloc(sizeof(struct xxx));
39        px->px = GcMalloc(sizeof(struct xxx));
40        px->py = GcMalloc(sizeof(struct yyy));
41        px->py->py = GcMalloc(sizeof(struct yyy));
42        printf("gcUsed = %2d\n", gcUsed);
43        /* verify that it collects properly */
44        GcSwapHeaps();
45        copy_xxx(&px);
46        printf("gcUsed = %2d\n", gcUsed);
47        /* create some garbage and collect it */
48        px->py->py = NULL;
49        GcSwapHeaps();
50        copy_xxx(&px);
51        printf("gcUsed = %2d\n", gcUsed);
52        /* create a shared structure and perform gc */
53        px->px->py = px->py;
54        GcSwapHeaps();
55        copy_xxx(&px);
56        printf("gcUsed = %2d\n", gcUsed);
57        /* create a circular structure and perform gc */
58        px->py->py = px->py;
59        GcSwapHeaps();
60        copy_xxx(&px);
61        printf("gcUsed = %2d\n", gcUsed);
62        /* create circular garbage and collect it */
63        px->px->py = px->py = NULL;
64        GcSwapHeaps();
65        copy_xxx(&px);
66        printf("gcUsed = %2d\n", gcUsed);
67        /* release the heaps */
68        GcClose();
69        }
```

File *gctest.c* is a simple test program for the garbage collector. The basic idea is that we have a data structure (consisting of structures *xxx* and *yyy* hanging off of one or more high-level pointers, such as *px* (line 34). For each structure type, there is an ad hoc copy routine. These routines are *copy_xxx* and *copy_yyy*. Each routine calls *GcCopyForward* to copy the block if it hasn't already been copied. If it is copied, then similar treatment is applied to the pointers in that block.

The main program (lines 33–69) exercise the garbage collector by performing allocations and running the collector. If you run this under a debugger and watch the value of *gcUsed* you can verify that the space is actually being reclaimed properly.

CODE GENERATION FROM A PARSER

An easy way to implement a language is to translate its source code into an existing language, which also makes available all the capability of that language. This is a very common technique. For example, embedded SQL is done this way.

Suppose the above garbage collection scheme is to be implemented, but it is desired to generate the copy routines automatically, so as to reduce source code redundancy. One way would be to put the structure definitions in a separate header file, for example *recs.h*. This could be run through a preprocessor to generate a file of copy routines, *copy_recs.c*.

The relevance of this to productivity is that programmers don't have to manually edit the copy routines, thereby reducing the redundancy of the source code when garbage collection is used. The actual language to be input to the preprocessor could have been a custom-designed data-definition language, in which case the preprocessor could have been used to generate the C structure definitions as well. By letting C itself be the data-definition language, however, not only is this extra step avoided, but all the type-definition syntax of C is available for free.

struct.h is a "typical" file to be input to the code generator. It contains structure definitions for each type of structure that can be garbage collected.

```
 1 /* struct.h  application structures to be processed */
 2
 3 struct xxx {
 4 GC   struct xxx * px;
 5 GC   struct yyy * py[MAXN];
 6      int data;
 7      };
 8
 9 struct yyy {
10 GC   struct yyy * py;
11      int data;
12      };
13
```

codegen.c is the actual code generator:

```
 1 /* codegen.c  parse structures to generate ad-hoc GC routines */
 2
 3 #include <stdio.h>
 4 #include "..\lexan\lexan.h"
 5
 6 FILE * fin = NULL;
 7
 8 int lex_getc(){
 9     return getc(fin);
10     }
11
12 int err = 0;
13
14 #define SETERR(i) {err = (i); return;}
15
16 parseStruct(int iPass){
17     long n = 0;              /* pointer array size, if present */
```

```
18      char sname[100];        /* name of structure */
19      char ptype[100];        /* structure name of pointer */
20      char pname[100];        /* name of pointer */
21      err = 0;
22      /* parse struct keyword */
23      if (!SEE("struct")) SETERR(1);
24      lexan();
25      /* parse structure id */
26      if (token!=T_ID) SETERR(1);
27      strcpy(sname, tokstr);
28      lexan();
29      /* in first pass, gen forward declaration of routine */
30      if (iPass==0) printf(
31 "extern void copy_%s(struct %s *P);\n\n"
32              , sname
33              , sname
34              );
35      /* in second pass, gen first part of copy routine */
36      if (iPass==1) printf(
37 "void copy_%s(struct %s *P){\n\tif(GcCopyForward(&P,sizeof(*P))){\n"
38              , sname
39              , sname
40              );
41      /* get opening curly bracket */
42      if (token!='{') SETERR(1);
43      lexan();
44      /* for each element of structure */
45      while(1){
46              if (token==EOF) SETERR(1);
47              if (token=='}'){
48                      lexan();
49                      break;
50                      }
51              /* if it starts with the macro GC, we process it */
52              if (SEE("GC")){
53                      lexan();
54                      /* it better be a struct pointer */
55                      if (!SEE("struct")) SETERR(1);
56                      lexan();
57                      /* get the struct name it points to */
58                      if (token != T_ID) SETERR(1);
59                      strcpy(ptype, tokstr);
60                      lexan();
61                      if (token != '*') SETERR(1);
62                      lexan();
63                      /* get the name of the pointer */
64                      if (token != T_ID) SETERR(1);
65                      strcpy(pname, tokstr);
66                      lexan();
67                      /* if an array of pointers, do the right thing */
68                      if (token=='['){
69                              char buf[20];
70                              lexan();
71                              if (!(token==T_LONG || token==T_ID))
72                                      SETERR(1);
73                              /* gen copy loop on that array */
74                              if (iPass==1){
75                                      if (token==T_LONG)
```

```
 76                                              sprintf(buf,"%ld",token_long);
 77                                    else
 78                                           strcpy(buf,tokstr);
 79                                   printf(
 80                          "\t\t{\tint i;\n\t\t\tfor(i=0;i<%s;i++)\n"
 81                                          ,buf
 82                                          );
 83                                   printf(
 84                          "\t\t\t\tcopy_%s(&(P->%s[i]));\n"
 85                                          , ptype
 86                                          , pname
 87                                          );
 88                                   printf("\t\t\t}\n");
 89                                   }
 90                          lexan();
 91                          if (token!=']') SETERR(1);
 92                          lexan();
 93                          }
 94                  /* else it's a single pointer */
 95                  else {
 96                          /* gen copy on that pointer */
 97                          if (iPass==1) printf(
 98                          "\t\tcopy_%s(&(P->%s));\n"
 99                                          , ptype
100                                          , pname
101                                          );
102                          }
103                  }
104          /* scan over the next semicolon */
105          while(token!=EOF && token!=';') lexan();
106          if (token==';') lexan();
107          }
108      /* gen close of copy routine */
109      if (iPass==1) printf(
110          "\t\t}\n\t}\n\n"
111          );
112      }
113
114 void main(int argc, char **argv){
115      int iPass;
116      argc--; argv++;
117      if (argc<=0){
118          printf("Usage: codegen struct.h > struct.c\n");
119          return;
120          }
121      for (iPass = 0; iPass < 2; iPass++){
122          fin = fopen(argv[0],"r");
123          if (fin==NULL) return;
124          init_lexan();
125          err = 0;
126          while(!err && token!=EOF){
127                  parseStruct(iPass);
128                  if (token==';') lexan();
129                  }
130          fclose(fin);
131          }
132      }
```

Its central routine is *parseStruct*, which parses a structure definition. Routine *main* calls it repeatedly to parse all the structures in the input file. The whole process is performed in two passes, so that only forward declarations of the routines are generated in pass 0, and the real routines are generated in pass 1. (Parsing the input twice is a simple technique that saves us having to build data structure.)

Following is a file of code generated by running the command *codegen struct.h > struct.c*:

```
 1 extern void copy_xxx(struct xxx *P);
 2
 3 extern void copy_yyy(struct yyy *P);
 4
 5 void copy_xxx(struct xxx *P){
 6     if(GcCopyForward(&P,sizeof(*P))){
 7             copy_xxx(&(P->px));
 8             {       int i;
 9                     for(i=0;i<MAXN;i++)
10                             copy_yyy(&(P->py[i]));
11             }
12     }
13   }
14
15 void copy_yyy(struct yyy *P){
16     if(GcCopyForward(&P,sizeof(*P))){
17             copy_yyy(&(P->py));
18     }
19   }
20
21
```

CONCLUSION

If data and programs can be looked at as the same thing, then the job of data can sometimes be done by interpreted or compiled programs. If data must be used, a garbage collector can reduce the source code redundancy and thus the maintenance cost.

5

Method

Methodologies scare me, because they are so appealing and at the same time so seemingly out of touch with the reality of programming. Nevertheless, I have been asked enough times if there is a method to what I do to convince me that some sort of cookbook approach might be helpful.

At the same time, while I care very much about software productivity, re-use, software quality, and so on, and I think the ideas in this book represent a significant contribution, I'm not sure I want to enter that wooly debate.

In any case, here is my method, cheekily christened the *Linguistic Methodology* because it depends on looking at information in linguistic terms. It consists of identifying the different kinds of information input to a system and asking the following questions:

Q. *What* is done with the information, and how much working storage is needed to do it? A good way to think of this working storage is as a set of *place markers* that you need so as to keep track of where you are in the information structure as you work.

A. None, you just copy the information:
Then it is in the linear class.
It can be represented in data structure.
It can be represented in any programming language.

A. You need to cycle around in the information, so you need just a few place markers (to keep track of your alternative paths):

Then it is in the finite-state class.

It can be represented in data structure, but programs that examine it will need a place marker, because it is an FSM.

It can be represented in any programming language, finite-state, stack, or parallel.

A. You need a pushdown stack of place markers:

Then the information is in the stack class.

If represented in data structure, programs that examine it will require a pushdown stack of place markers, whether explicit, if the language is finite-state, or implicit, if the language is stack or parallel. It can be represented in any stack or parallel language.

A. You need a random set of place markers:

Then the information is in the parallel class.

If represented in data structure, programs that examine it will require a random collection of place markers—whether explicit, if the language is finite-state or stack, or implicit, if the language is parallel.

It can be represented in a parallel language.

Q. *When* is the information acquired?

A. At run time:

The information can be represented in data structure. This will entail writing programs to interpret it.

It can be represented in an interpreted language of the proper level, if one is available.

It can be represented in a compiled language of the proper level if one is available and run-time compilation and linking is possible. This takes time on the order of seconds to compile and link, but subsequent speed is high.

A. At installation time:

The information can be represented in data structure. This will entail writing programs to interpret it.

It can be represented in an interpreted language of the proper level, if one is available.

It can be represented in a compiled language of the proper level if one is available and installation time compilation and linking are possible.

A. At development time:

The information can be represented in data structure. This entails not only writing programs to interpret the data structure, but programs to create the data structure.

It can be represented in an interpreted language of the proper level.

It can be represented in a compiled language of the proper level, for highest performance.

Q. *Who* provides the information?

A. Persons whose programming skill (at the necessary language level) can be utilized:
    The information can be acquired by having them write programs.

A. Other persons:
    A user-interface program must be written to solicit the information and encode it in the chosen representation.

EXAMPLE: DESIGN OF USER-INTERFACE SOFTWARE

Imagine designing a hypothetical on-line database query system. We identify each kind of information that goes into it and ask the questions about each one. The principal kinds of information are the layout of the screens, the sequential operation flow, and the actual run-time database.

What is the content of the screen layout? There may be a large number of screens, on the order of a hundred. Each screen typically has a fixed set of fields, but some may have a scrolled list of fields. Each field has a position, width, type, validation criteria, and a database field to which it refers. If screens needed to contain only fixed fields, their descriptions would be linear:

```
FIELD A
FIELD B
FIELD C
```

If screens also needed to have scrolling regions of many identical lines, their description would be finite-state, due to the implied iteration:

```
FIELD A
FOR EACH SCROLLING REGION LINE I
   FIELD B[I]
   FIELD C[I]
END SCROLLING REGION
FIELD D
```

If the screens are to have common sub-screens shared by many screens, the description is at the stack level:

```
FIELD A
INCLUDE SUBSCREEN1
FIELD C
```

because any program to paint or read the description needs a stack to keep track of the possible nested INCLUDES.

The *when* question asks at what time is the screen layout information acquired—whether at run-time or development time (or installation time). Typically, it is acquired during or prior to development. This implies that precompiling is an optional representation technique. If the information is finite-state, it can be precompiled into just about any computer language. On the other hand, the information can also be represented as a data structure having a run-time interpreter, and that interpreter will not require a stack. If the information is acquired at run-time, that does not necessarily rule out a pre-compiled approach, as it may be possible to dynamically compile a screen and dynamically link it.

The *who* question asks what kind of interface is required to capture the information. If a programmer is capturing the information, it may be that a simple text editor is sufficient. On the other hand, if the person needs careful guidance, a more sophisticated screen-design program may have to be provided, with its own set of design questions.

EXAMPLE: COMPUTER GRAPHICS EVOLUTION

Computer graphics is a domain rich in shifting answers to the representation questions. Originally, displays were produced as line drawings generated by display procedures called many times per second. These display procedures were simply programs written in the native instruction set of a general-purpose computer. Later, to offload the computer, specialized processors (the IBM 2250, for example) were created. They would refresh from a "display list" made up of very simple instructions such as Point(x,y), Line(x,y), and Jump(location). This is reduction in schematic level from a parallel-level instruction set (that could take advantage of heap storage) to a linear instruction set (having no auxiliary registers and no conditional branching). The application program in the host computer had to encode each desired image in this linear language and write it to the device, whereas before the application program was itself the encoding (Figure 5.1).

There were many competing suppliers of display generation equipment, and a primary evolution direction was to make the display list instruction set more "intelligent." Subroutine call instructions were added, so that a subpicture represented by a single display list segment could be replicated many places throughout an image. General-purpose registers were added, and also arithmetic instructions, so that scaling and rotation could be done in the display generator. Conditional jumps and facilities to read external inputs such as joysticks were added. What was originally just linear data was being elevated in the linguistic hierarchy to the stack level.

In the 1970s, Alan Kay's Smalltalk appeared. It was an interpreted instruction set featuring object-oriented programming (OOP) and so the hierarchy had reached the parallel level. This instruction set, with an acceptable surface syntax, was powerful enough to do the whole job with no need for a host computer.

Also at this time raster displays came into common use, so the need for high-speed refresh went away, freeing the display processor to do host functions. As the distinction between host and display processor began to disappear, so did the justification for special purpose display-list instruction sets. Nevertheless,

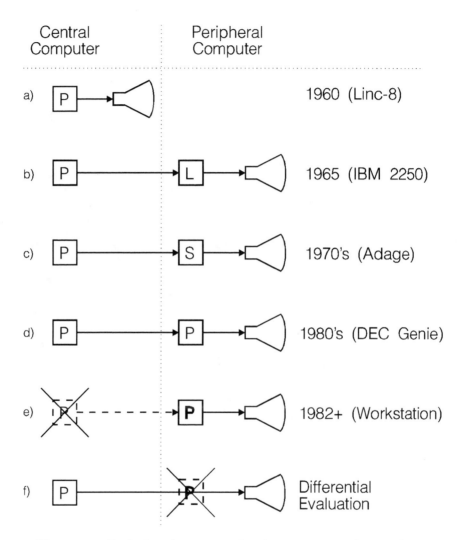

Figure 5.1. Evolution of representations in computer graphics: (a) Originally the display device had no memory and was attached directly to the host computer (parallel-level instruction set). (b) Refresh was offloaded to the display processor with a linear instruction set (no conditional branching). (c) and (d) The display processor instruction set evolves to parallel level again (the wheel of reincarnation). (e) The host computer becomes redundant, starting the cycle over again. (f) If differential evaluation is used, the cycle is broken by removing the need to offload the host.

even into the 1980s there were cases of machines having separate host/display processors and special instruction sets for graphics.

Now the best way is to have the host computer simply call subroutines to directly draw the desired shapes in the image buffer. In this way, the display list's role is played by a instruction sequence in the host computer's native instruction set that just happened to have been written by a person (with a compiler's help). The display list doesn't have to be dynamic data because its own conditionals and calculations account for all desired variations. Notice how easy it is to reflect real-time application data in the display. The data is just directly referenced and used. It doesn't have to be moved into some register or data structure.

One feature of the old direct-refresh devices was dynamic image motion in response to real-time data changes. Although this is more difficult to program with raster displays, differential execution is a helpful technology.

CONCLUSION

This method differs from others in that it is not *data centered*, and it does not directly try to identify objects of discourse. I feel that data-centered approaches tend to result in too much run-time data structure, and consequently redundant source code—in a word, the *object-action* model.

I don't know if this approach will catch on. Now and again I see signs that it is, such as that people seem to need code generators to write object-oriented programs, or that many successful vendor software packages started in someone's garage where they had to be productive, or else.

As these trends develop, the next few years should prove interesting. On the one hand, I expect the object-oriented trend to play itself out as a good idea, but far from final—perhaps pragmatism will step in behind it. On the other hand, some new butterfly, such as "visual programming," may float across our line of sight and lead us on another wild chase.

Can we afford it?

Appendix A. Graphical Utilities

An old trick used in military applications is to use fixed point fractions in place of floating point arithmetic. It has the speed of integers, but can represent fractional quantities. These two files define FIXP, a 32-bit numeric type in which the ten low-order bits are the fraction. They can be added and subtracted like ordinary integers. They can be multiplied with the *FIXTIMES(a,b)* macro. There are trigonometric functions *fsin(a)* and *fcos(a)* that take an angle in integer degrees and return a fixed-point fraction.

```
 1 /* fastmath.h math package using fixed-point fractions */
 2
 3 typedef long FIXP;
 4
 5 #define TOFIXP(v)((long)((v)*1024))
 6 #define TOLONG(v)((long)((v)>>10))
 7 #define FIXTIMES(a,b)(((a)*(b))>>10)
 8
 9 extern long fsin(int d);
10 extern long fcos(int d);
11
```

```
 1 /* fastmath.c  math package using fixed-point fractions */
 2
 3 #include "fastmath.h"
 4 #include <math.h>
 5
 6 #define RADPERDEG (3.1415926535 / 180.0)
 7
 8 static int initsin_p = 0;
```

```
 9
10  static long sintab[361];
11
12  static void init_sintab(){
13      int i; long d;
14      for (i = 0; i < 91; i++){
15              d = TOFIXP(sin(i * RADPERDEG));
16              sintab[i] = d;
17              sintab[180 - i] =  d;
18              sintab[180 + i] = -d;
19              sintab[360 - i] = -d;
20              }
21      }
22
23  long fsin(int d){
24      if (!initsin_p){
25              init_sintab();
26              initsin_p = 1;
27              }
28      while (d>=360) d-=360;
29      while (d<0) d+=360;
30      return(sintab[d]);
31      }
32
33  long fcos(int d){
34      return(fsin(d+90));
35      }
```

The following three files contain DOS- and EGA-specific graphical primitive routines to draw lines, rectangles, and text by the XOR method. They have been highly optimized. XORLINE, in particular, is an example of using macros in conjunction with loop unrolling to achieve low cycle-count with decent maintainability.

For those unfamiliar with the function of an EGA graphic card, drawing a pixel requires a few steps. The screen is 640 by 350 4-bit pixels organized as four planes. Each plane has 8 pixels per byte. When the card's registers are configured, you only need to touch a byte in the first plane, and all four planes are modified. Setting a register on the card takes two *out* instructions, one to say which register you want to modify, and one to supply the value. The steps are:

1. The 4-bit color code must be stored in the set–reset (SR) registers.
2. All 4 bits of color must be enabled (unless you want to draw on less than all 4-bit planes).
3. The arithmetic logic unit (ALU) operation code must be set to 3, the code for XOR.
4. The mask register must be set to the 8-pixel bit pattern you wish to XOR into the image byte.
5. A read-write cycle must be performed against the byte. I use (*p = 1) where p is a pointer to the image byte. (The 1 is ignored. The act of reading and writing causes the card's machinery to function, XORing the color into the 4-bit planes in the pattern specified by the mask register.) In engineers' slang this is called *bit banging*.

This isn't all done on every pixel. The setup is done once. Then the mask register is selected, and the inner loop consists of setting the mask register and banging the image bytes over and over.

```
 1 /* xorline.c */
 2
 3 #include <stdio.h>
 4 #include <graph.h>
 5 #include <dos.h>
 6
 7 /* extern void outp(int port,int val);/**/
 8 extern unsigned int _rotl(unsigned int mask,int val);
 9 extern unsigned int _rotr(unsigned int mask,int val);
10
11 #if 0        /* if /Ox compile flag is used, this must not be used */
12 #pragma intrinsic(outp,_rotr,_rotl)
13 #endif
14
15 #define SETVIDREG(reg,val){outp(0x3ce,(reg)); outp(0x3cf,(val));}
16 #define SETVIDALU(alu) SETVIDREG(3,(alu)<<3)         /* 0:store 1:and 2:or 3:xor */
17 #define SETVIDMODE(mode) SETVIDREG(5,mode)
18 #define SETVIDSR(color) SETVIDREG(0,color)
19 #define SETVIDSRENB(mask) SETVIDREG(1,mask)
20 #define SETVIDMASK(mask) SETVIDREG(8,mask)
21
22 static char far * fm_screen = (char far *)0xa0000000;
23
24 #define OUTMASK outp(0x3cf,mask)
25 #define INCX {sum += dy; mask=_rotr(mask,1); if ((signed int)mask<0) p++; OUTMASK;}
26 #define INCY {sum -= dx; p+=BYTES_PER_LINE;}
27 #define DECX {sum -= dy; if ((signed int)mask<0) p--; mask=_rotl(mask,1); OUTMASK;}
28 #define DECY {sum += dx; p-=BYTES_PER_LINE;}
29 #define SETPIX (*p |= 1)
30 #define STEP4 {if (n>=4){STEP; STEP; STEP; STEP; n-= 4;}}
31 #define STEP1 {if (n<=0) break; STEP; n--;}
32 #define STEPFOR for (;;){STEP4; STEP1;}
33 #define STEP
34
35 #define BYTES_PER_LINE 80
36
37 xorline(x0,y0,x1,y1,color){
38     int dx = x1 - x0;
39     int dy = y1 - y0;
40     int x = x0;
41     int y = y0;
42     register int sum = 0;
43     register unsigned int mask = 0x8080>>(x & 7);
44     char far * p = fm_screen + BYTES_PER_LINE*y + (x>>3);
45     int n;
46
47     SETVIDSR(color);
48     SETVIDSRENB(15);
49     SETVIDALU(3);
50     SETVIDMASK(255);
51     OUTMASK;
```

```
52          /* THIS IS BASED ON THE IDEA THAT  DX * DY  =  DY * DX  */
53          /* IF BOTH DX AND DY ARE POSITIVE THEN
54                  SUM = NX * DY - NY * DX SHOULD BE 0 */
55       if (dx >= 0){
56                  /* SOUTHEAST: DX>=0 && DY>=0 */
57               if (dy >= 0){
58                      /* EAST-SOUTHEAST */
59                      if (dx >= dy){
60                              sum -= dx/2;
61                              n = dx;
62 #undef STEP
63 #define STEP {SETPIX; INCX; if (sum>=0) INCY;}
64                              STEPFOR;
65                              }
66                      /* SOUTH-SOUTHEAST */
67                      else {
68                              sum += dy/2;
69                              n = dy;
70 #undef STEP
71 #define STEP {SETPIX; INCY; if (sum<=0) INCX;}
72                              STEPFOR;
73                              }
74                      }
75               /* NORTHEAST: DX>=0 && DY<0 */
76               else {
77                      /* EAST-NORTHEAST */
78                      if (dx >= -dy){
79                              sum += dx/2;
80                              n = dx;
81 #undef STEP
82 #define STEP {SETPIX; INCX; if (sum<=0) DECY;}
83                              STEPFOR;
84                              }
85                      /* NORTH-NORTHEAST */
86                      else {
87                              sum += dy/2;
88                              n = -dy;
89 #undef STEP
90 #define STEP {SETPIX; DECY; if (sum>=0) INCX;}
91                              STEPFOR;
92                              }
93                      }
94               }
95       else {
96               /* SOUTHWEST: DX<0 && DY>=0 */
97               if (dy >= 0){
98                      /* WEST-SOUTHWEST */
99                      if (dx <= -dy){
100                             sum -= dx/2;
101                             n = -dx;
102 #undef STEP
103 #define STEP {SETPIX; DECX; if (sum<=0) INCY;}
104                             STEPFOR;
105                             }
106                     /* SOUTH-SOUTHWEST */
107                     else {
108                             sum -= dy/2;
109                             n = dy;
```

```
110 #undef STEP
111 #define STEP {SETPIX; INCY; if (sum>=0) DECX;}
112                              STEPFOR;
113                              }
114                      }
115             /* NORTHWEST: DX<0 && DY<0 */
116           else {
117                      /* WEST-NORTHWEST */
118                      if (dx <= dy){
119                              sum += dx/2;
120                              n = -dx;
121 #undef STEP
122 #define STEP {SETPIX; DECX; if (sum>=0) DECY;}
123                              STEPFOR;
124                              }
125                      /* NORTH-NORTHWEST */
126                      else {
127                              sum -= dy/2;
128                              n = -dy;
129 #undef STEP
130 #define STEP {SETPIX; DECY; if (sum<=0) DECX;}
131                              STEPFOR;
132                              }
133                      }
134              }
135     SETVIDMASK(255);
136     SETVIDSR(0);
137     SETVIDSRENB(0);
138     SETVIDALU(0);
139     }
```

```
 1 /* xorrect.c */
 2
 3 #include <stdlib.h>
 4 #include <stdio.h>
 5 #include <graph.h>
 6 #include <dos.h>
 7
 8 #define SETVIDREG(reg,val){outp(0x3ce,(reg)); outp(0x3cf,(val));}
 9 #define SETVIDALU(alu) SETVIDREG(3,(alu)<<3)          /* 0:store 1:and 2:or 3:xor */
10 #define SETVIDMODE(mode) SETVIDREG(5,mode)
11 #define SETVIDMODE(mode) SETVIDREG(5,mode)
12 #define SETVIDSR(color) SETVIDREG(0,color)
13 #define SETVIDSRENB(mask) SETVIDREG(1,mask)
14 #define SETVIDMASK(mask) SETVIDREG(8,mask)
15
16 static char far * fm_screen = (char far *)0xa0000000;
17
18 xorrect(x0,y0,x1,y1,color){
19     char far * p0 = fm_screen + 80*y0 + (x0>>3);
20     SETVIDSR(color);
21     SETVIDSRENB(15);
22     SETVIDALU(3);
23     SETVIDMASK(255);
24     /* IF CONTAINED IN A SINGLE BYTE */
25     if ((x0 & -8)==(x1 & -8)){
```

```
26                  int iy;
27                  /* GET MASK FOR THE BYTE */
28                  unsigned char mask = (0xff>>(x0 & 7)) & ~(0xff>>(x1 & 7));
29                  /* FOR EACH SCAN LINE */
30                  outp(0x3cf,mask);
31                  for (iy=y0; iy<y1; iy++, p0 += 80){
32                          /* BANG OUT BYTE */
33                          p0[0] |= 1;
34                          }
35                  }
36      /* ELSE MULTI_BYTE */
37      else {
38                  /* GET MASK FOR FIRST AND LAST BYTES */
39                  unsigned char mask = (0xff >> (x0 & 7));
40                  unsigned char mask1 = ~(0xff >> (x1 & 7));
41                  int ix,iy;
42                  /* FOR EACH SCAN LINE */
43                  for (iy=y0; iy<y1; iy++, p0 += 80){
44                          unsigned char far * p = p0;
45                          /* BANG OUT FIRST BYTE */
46                          outp(0x3cf,mask); *p++ |= 1;
47                          /* INTERMEDIATE BYTES */
48                          outp(0x3cf,0xff);
49                          for (ix = (x0>>3)+1; ix < (x1>>3); ix++){
50                                  *p++ |= 1;
51                                  }
52                          /* LAST BYTE */
53                          outp(0x3cf,mask1); *p++ |= 1;
54                          }
55                  }
56      SETVIDMASK(255);
57      SETVIDSR(0);
58      SETVIDSRENB(0);
59      SETVIDALU(0);
60      }
61
62  #if 0
63  main(){
64      int x=0,y=0,dx=0,dy=0,c,color=14;
65      int i;
66      _setvideomode(_ERESCOLOR);
67      while(1){
68              xorrect(x,y,x+dx,y+dy,color);
69              c = getch();
70              xorrect(x,y,x+dx,y+dy,color);
71              if (0);
72              else if (c=='l') x--;
73              else if (c=='r') x++;
74              else if (c=='u') y--;
75              else if (c=='d') y++;
76              else if (c=='b'){dx++; dy++;}
77              else if (c=='s'){dx--; dy--;}
78              else if (c=='q') break;
79              }
80      _setvideomode(_DEFAULTMODE);
81      }
82  #endif
```

```
 1  /* xortext.c */
 2
 3  #include <stdlib.h>
 4  #include <stdio.h>
 5  #include <graph.h>
 6  #include <dos.h>
 7
 8  #if 0
 9  extern void outp(int port,int val);
10  extern unsigned int _rotl(unsigned int mask,int val);
11  extern unsigned int _rotr(unsigned int mask,int val);
12
13  #pragma intrinsic(outp,_rotr,_rotl)
14  #endif
15
16  static int height = 9;
17
18  typedef unsigned char font_char[9];
19  #define ____ 0x0
20  #define ___1 0x1
21  #define __1_ 0x2
22  #define __11 0x3
23  #define _1__ 0x4
24  #define _1_1 0x5
25  #define _11_ 0x6
26  #define _111 0x7
27  #define 1___ 0x8
28  #define 1__1 0x9
29  #define 1_1_ 0xa
30  #define 1_11 0xb
31  #define 11__ 0xc
32  #define 11_1 0xd
33  #define 111_ 0xe
34  #define 1111 0xf
35  #define S(a,b)(a<<4 | b)
36
37  static font_char font[128] = {
38  /* 0 */
39      {0,0,0,0,0,0,0,0,0}
40      ,{0,0,0,0,0,0,0,0,0}
41      ,{0,0,0,0,0,0,0,0,0}
42      ,{0,0,0,0,0,0,0,0,0}
43      ,{0,0,0,0,0,0,0,0,0}
44      ,{0,0,0,0,0,0,0,0,0}
45      ,{0,0,0,0,0,0,0,0,0}
46      ,{0,0,0,0,0,0,0,0,0}
47      ,{0,0,0,0,0,0,0,0,0}
48      ,{0,0,0,0,0,0,0,0,0}
49      ,{0,0,0,0,0,0,0,0,0}
50      ,{0,0,0,0,0,0,0,0,0}
51      ,{0,0,0,0,0,0,0,0,0}
52      ,{0,0,0,0,0,0,0,0,0}
53      ,{0,0,0,0,0,0,0,0,0}
54      ,{0,0,0,0,0,0,0,0,0}
55  /* 0x10 */
56      ,{0,0,0,0,0,0,0,0,0}
57      ,{0,0,0,0,0,0,0,0,0}
```

```
58      ,{0,0,0,0,0,0,0,0,0,0}
59      ,{0,0,0,0,0,0,0,0,0,0}
60      ,{0,0,0,0,0,0,0,0,0,0}
61      ,{0,0,0,0,0,0,0,0,0,0}
62      ,{0,0,0,0,0,0,0,0,0,0}
63      ,{0,0,0,0,0,0,0,0,0,0}
64      ,{0,0,0,0,0,0,0,0,0,0}
65      ,{0,0,0,0,0,0,0,0,0,0}
66      ,{0,0,0,0,0,0,0,0,0,0}
67      ,{0,0,0,0,0,0,0,0,0,0}
68      ,{0,0,0,0,0,0,0,0,0,0}
69      ,{0,0,0,0,0,0,0,0,0,0}
70      ,{0,0,0,0,0,0,0,0,0,0}
71      ,{0,0,0,0,0,0,0,0,0,0}
72 /* 0x20 */
73 /* space */
74        ,{S(____,____),
75      S(____,____),
76      S(____,____),
77      S(____,____),
78      S(____,____),
79      S(____,____),
80      S(____,____),
81      S(____,____),
82      S(____,____)
83      }
84 /* ! */
85        ,{S(__11,____),
86      S(_111,1___),
87      S(_111,1___),
88      S(__11,____),
89      S(__11,____),
90      S(__11,____),
91      S(____,____),
92      S(_111,1___),
93      S(_111,1___)
94      }
95 /* " */
96        ,{S(_11_,11__),
97      S(_11_,11__),
98      S(____,____),
99      S(____,____),
100     S(____,____),
101     S(____,____),
102     S(____,____),
103     S(____,____),
104     S(____,____)
105     }
106 /* # */
107       ,{S(_11_,11__),
108     S(_11_,11__),
109     S(1111,111_),
110     S(_11_,11__),
111     S(_11_,11__),
112     S(_11_,11__),
113     S(1111,111_),
114     S(_11_,11__),
115     S(_11_,11__)
```

```
116      }
117 /* $ */
118        ,{S(__11,____),
119     S(_111,1___),
120     S(11__,11__),
121     S(_11_,____),
122     S(__11,____),
123     S(___1,1___),
124     S(11__,11__),
125     S(_111,1___),
126     S(__11,____)
127      }
128 /* & */
129        ,{S(____,____),
130     S(11__,__1_),
131     S(11__,_11_),
132     S(____,11__),
133     S(___1,1___),
134     S(__11,____),
135     S(_11_,____),
136     S(11__,_11_),
137     S(1___,_11_)
138      }

. . . . .

1069 /* z */
1070       ,{S(____,____),
1071    S(____,____),
1072    S(____,____),
1073    S(_111,111_),
1074    S(____,11__),
1075    S(___1,1___),
1076    S(__11,____),
1077    S(_11_,____),
1078    S(_111,111_)
1079     }
1080 /* { */
1081       ,{S(____,11__),
1082    S(___1,1___),
1083    S(__11,____),
1084    S(__11,____),
1085    S(_11_,____),
1086    S(__11,____),
1087    S(__11,____),
1088    S(___1,1___),
1089    S(____,11__)
1090     }
1091 /* | */
1092       ,{S(___1,1___),
1093    S(___1,1___),
1094    S(___1,1___),
1095    S(___1,1___),
1096    S(____,____),
1097    S(___1,1___),
1098    S(___1,1___),
1099    S(___1,1___),
1100    S(___1,1___)
```

```
1101      }
1102 /* } */
1103      ,{S(__11,____),
1104    S(___1,1___),
1105    S(____,11__),
1106    S(____,11__),
1107    S(____,_11_),
1108    S(____,11__),
1109    S(____,11__),
1110    S(___1,1___),
1111    S(__11,____)
1112      }
1113 /* ~ */
1114       ,{S(_111,_11_),
1115    S(11_1,11__),
1116    S(____,____),
1117    S(____,____),
1118    S(____,____),
1119    S(____,____),
1120    S(____,____),
1121    S(____,____),
1122    S(____,____)
1123      }
1124 /* del */
1125       ,{S(1111,1111),
1126    S(1111,1111),
1127    S(1111,1111),
1128    S(1111,1111),
1129    S(1111,1111),
1130    S(1111,1111),
1131    S(1111,1111),
1132    S(1111,1111),
1133    S(1111,1111)
1134      }
1135      };
1136
1137 #define SETVIDREG(reg,val){outp(0x3ce,(reg)); outp(0x3cf,(val));}
1138 #define SETVIDALU(alu) SETVIDREG(3,(alu)<<3)          /* 0:store 1:and 2:or 3:xor */
1139 #define SETVIDMODE(mode) SETVIDREG(5,mode)
1140 #define SETVIDMODE(mode) SETVIDREG(5,mode)
1141 #define SETVIDSR(color) SETVIDREG(0,color)
1142 #define SETVIDSRENB(mask) SETVIDREG(1,mask)
1143 #define SETVIDMASK(mask) SETVIDREG(8,mask)
1144
1145 static char far * fm_screen = (char far *)0xa0000000;
1146
1147 xortext(x0,y0,s,color)char * s;{
1148     char far * p0 = fm_screen + 80*y0 + (x0>>3);
1149     unsigned char shift = x0 & 7;
1150     register unsigned short mask;
1151     SETVIDSR(color);
1152     SETVIDSRENB(15);
1153     SETVIDALU(3);
1154     SETVIDMASK(255);
1155     /* FOR EACH CHARACTER */
1156     for (; *s; s++, p0++){
1157             int iy;
1158             unsigned char * pchar;
```

```
1159                 register char far * p;
1160                 /* FOR EACH SCAN LINE */
1161                 for (   p=p0, pchar=font[*s], iy=0;
1162                         iy<height;
1163                         iy++, pchar++, p+=80
1164                         ){
1165                         /* GET SCAN LINE AS 16 BITS */
1166                         mask = *pchar;
1167                         /* ROTATE RIGHTMOST BITS INTO HIGH BYTE */
1168                         mask = _rotr(mask,shift);
1169                         /* BANG OUT LOW BYTE, THEN HIGH BYTE */
1170                         outp(0x3cf,(unsigned char)mask); p[0] |= 1;
1171                         outp(0x3cf,(unsigned char)(mask>>8)); p[1] |= 1;
1172                         }
1173             }
1174     SETVIDMASK(255);
1175     SETVIDSR(0);
1176     SETVIDSRENB(0);
1177     SETVIDALU(0);
1178     }
1179
1180 #if 0
1181 void main(){
1182     int x=0,y=0,c,color=14;
1183     int i;
1184     char buf0[200];
1185     char buf1[200];
1186     for (i=0; i<64; i++) buf0[i] = i;
1187     buf0[0] = 1;
1188     buf0[i] = 0;
1189     for (i=0; i<64; i++) buf1[i] = i+64;
1190     buf1[i] = 0;
1191     _setvideomode(_ERESCOLOR);
1192     while(1){
1193             xortext(x,y,buf0,color);
1194             xortext(x,y+10,buf1,color);
1195             c = getch();
1196             xortext(x,y,buf0,color);
1197             xortext(x,y+10,buf1,color);
1198             if (0);
1199             else if (c=='l') x--;
1200             else if (c=='r') x++;
1201             else if (c=='u') y--;
1202             else if (c=='d') y++;
1203             else if (c=='q') break;
1204             }
1205     _setvideomode(_DEFAULTMODE);
1206     }
1207 #endif
```

Appendix B. CIM Simulation—Original

Following are some useful global definitions:

```
1 /* ignl.h global definitions */
2
3 #define FALSE 0
4 #define TRUE  1
5
6 #define MALLOC malloc
7
```

The list cluster provides *ILST*, a linked-list data type. A list cell contains a *next* pointer to the next cell (or NULL), and a *thing* pointer to its contents. The operations are *create, append, first, next, nth, length,* and *delete*:

```
1 /* ilst.h list cluster definitions */
2
3 typedef struct ilst_struct {          /* list cell structure */
4    struct ilst_struct * next;         /* pointer to next cell */
5    void * thing;                      /* pointer to thing in cell */
6    } * ILST ;
7
8 /* list cluster access macros */
9
10 #define ILST_CREATE (NULL)
11
12 #define ILST_APPEND(list,thing) ((list)=ilst_append((list),thing))
13
14 #define ILST_FIRST(list) (((ILST)(list))->thing)
```

```
15
16 #define ILST_NEXT(list,thing) (ilst_next((list),(thing)))
17
18 #define ILST_NTH(list,n) (ilst_nth((list),n))
19
20 #define ILST_LENGTH(list) (ilst_length(list))
21
22 #define ILST_DELETE(list,thing) ((list)=ilst_delete((list),thing))
23
24 /* list cluster function externs */
25
26 extern ILST ilst_append();
27 extern void *      ilst_next();
28 extern void *      ilst_nth();
29 extern int  ilst_length();
30 extern ILST ilst_delete();
```

The transaction cluster defines ITRN, a transaction datatype. It contains only a transaction code. Actual transactions are subclassed from it (manually, because this is written in C) by appending specific data fields. The generic operations are put, get, and examine. The specific transaction records are also defined here:

```
 1 /* itrn.h general and application-specific transaction definitions */
 2
 3 /* ITRN is the 'superclass' of all transactions */
 4 typedef struct itrn_struct {
 5     int code;                /* the transaction code */
 6     } * ITRN;
 7
 8 /* externs of the transaction-processing cluster routines */
 9
10 extern void itrn_put();     /* put transaction in queue */
11 extern ITRN itrn_get();     /* get transaction from queue */
12 extern ITRN itrn_examine(); /* get transaction but leave it in queue */
13
14 typedef struct {    /* job request transaction */
15     int code;                /* transaction code */
16     int jobid;               /* job id */
17     } itrn_reqjob_t;
18
19 typedef struct {    /* job completion transaction */
20     int code;                /* transaction code */
21     int jobid;               /* job id */
22     } itrn_ackjob_t;
23
24 typedef struct {    /* operation request transaction */
25     int code;                /* transaction code */
26     int jobid;               /* job id */
27     int opid;                /* operation id */
28     } itrn_reqop_t;
29
30 typedef struct {    /* operation completion transaction */
31     int code;                /* transaction code */
```

```
32      int jobid;               /* job id */
33      int opid;                /* operation id */
34      } itrn_ackop_t;
35
36 typedef struct {     /* material handling move request transaction */
37      int code;                /* transaction code */
38      int mvid;                /* move id */
39      } itrn_reqmh_t;
40
41 typedef struct {     /* material handling move completion transaction */
42      int code;                /* transaction code */
43      int mvid;                /* move id */
44      } itrn_ackmh_t;
45
46 typedef struct {     /* device task request transaction */
47      int code;                /* transaction code */
48      int tskid;               /* task id */
49      } itrn_reqtsk_t;
50
51 typedef struct {     /* device task completion transaction */
52      int code;                /* transaction code */
53      int tskid;               /* task id */
54      } itrn_acktsk_t;
```

The specific transaction code definitions are given in the following file:

```
1 /* itrndef.h application transaction code definitions */
2
3 #define ISCH_REQJOB 101      /* job request */
4
5 #define ISCH_ACKJOB 102      /* job completion */
6
7 #define ITC_REQOP   201      /* operation request */
8
9 #define ITC_ACKOP   202      /* operation completion */
10
11 #define IMH_REQMOVE 301      /* material handling move request */
12
13 #define IMH_ACKMOVE 302      /* material handling move completion */
14
15 #define IDEV_REQTSK 401      /* device task request */
16
17 #define IDEV_ACKTSK 402      /* device task completion */
18
```

main.c contains the top level of the simulation, including the transaction dispatch loop:

```
1 /* main.c */
2
3 #include <stdio.h>
4 #include "ignl.h"
```

```
 5 #include "ilst.h"
 6 #include "itrn.h"
 7 #include "itrndef.h"
 8
 9 typedef int (*func_t)();
10
11 typedef struct itrn_tbl_struct {
12     int code;
13     func_t hndlr;
14     } itrn_tbl_t;
15
16 extern int isch_hndlr();
17 extern int itc_hndlr();
18 extern int imh_hndlr();
19 extern int idev_hndlr();
20
21 int nextjob;
22 int jobs_started, jobs_completed;
23
24 #define in_process_jobs (jobs_started - jobs_completed)
25
26 #define MAXJOBS 100
27
28 int newjobs(){
29     itrn_reqjob_t * preq;
30     while(jobs_started < MAXJOBS && in_process_jobs < 10){
31             preq = (itrn_reqjob_t*)MALLOC(sizeof(itrn_reqjob_t));
32             preq->code = ISCH_REQJOB;
33             preq->jobid = nextjob++;
34             itrn_put(preq);
35             jobs_started++;
36             }
37     }
38
39 int debug=1;
40
41 int main_hndlr(ptrn) ITRN ptrn;{
42     int err = FALSE;
43     if (ptrn->code==ISCH_ACKJOB){
44             jobs_completed++;
45             if (debug){
46                     printf("Ack Job %d\n",((itrn_ackjob_t*)ptrn)->jobid);
47                     }
48             newjobs();
49             }
50     free(ptrn);
51     return(err);
52     }
53
54 itrn_tbl_t itrn_tbl[] = {
55     {ISCH_REQJOB,    isch_hndlr},
56     {ISCH_ACKJOB,    main_hndlr},
57     {ITC_REQOP,      itc_hndlr},
58     {ITC_ACKOP,      isch_hndlr},
59     {IMH_REQMOVE,    imh_hndlr},
60     {IMH_ACKMOVE,    itc_hndlr},
61     {IDEV_REQTSK,    idev_hndlr},
62     {IDEV_ACKTSK,    itc_hndlr},
```

```
63      {0,NULL}
64      };
65
66 ITRN ptrn;
67
68 main(argc,argv) char ** argv;{
69      itrn_tbl_t * pt;
70      /* INIT TRANSACTION HANDLERS */
71      /* REQUEST FIRST JOBS */
72      newjobs();
73      /* LOOP FOREVER */
74      while(TRUE){
75              /* GET NEXT TRANSACTION */
76              ptrn = itrn_get();
77              if (ptrn==NULL) break;
78              /* IF NO MORE TRANSACTIONS, QUIT */
79              /* DISPATCH TO PROPER HANDLER */
80              for (pt = itrn_tbl; pt->code; pt++){
81                      if (pt->code==ptrn->code){
82                              if (pt->hndlr != NULL){
83                                      (*pt->hndlr)(ptrn);
84                              }
85                              break;
86                      }
87              }
88              if (!pt->code){
89                      /* UNRECOGNIZED CODE */
90                      fprintf(stderr,"Error - unrec transaction code %d\n"
91                              ,ptrn->code
92                              );
93              }
94      }
95      }
```

Lines 9–19 define the structure of the transaction dispatch table. Each entry associates a transaction code with the handler for that transaction.

The table itself is given in lines 54–64.

Variable *nextjob* is the next job number to be assigned. *jobs_started* and *jobs_completed* keep track of the number of jobs started and completed. Routine *newjobs()* is called periodically to request new jobs. In real life these come from outside.

Handler *main_hndlr(ptrn)* (lines 41–52) receives job completion acknowledgements, prints some output, and calls *newjobs()*.

The *main()* program simply calls *newjobs()* to start the ball rolling, and then falls into a transaction dispatch loop until the whole thing finishes.

The following file contains the transaction handlers for the schedule execution module. It keeps track of a list of jobs in process *(job_t)* and a list of batch operations *(bop_t)* for each job.

```
1 /* isch.c schedule execution transaction handler */
2
3 #include <stdio.h>
4 #include "ignl.h"
```

```
 5 #include "ilst.h"
 6 #include "itrn.h"
 7 #include "itrndef.h"
 8
 9 #if 0
10 On job request,
11     receive process plan
12     stick it into data base
13     create job structure
14
15 On batch operation complete
16     determine next batch operation to run
17             and send request to the task coordinator
18     If no more batch operations on job,
19             signal job completion
20 #endif
21
22 ILST joblist;
23
24 typedef struct {
25     int jobid;
26     ILST boplist;
27     int current_op;
28     } job_t;
29
30 typedef struct {
31     int triggered, complete;
32     } bop_t;
33
34 job_t * isch_findjob(jobid) int jobid;{
35     job_t * pjob;
36     for (pjob = ILST_FIRST(joblist);
37             pjob && pjob->jobid != jobid;
38             pjob = ILST_NEXT(joblist,pjob)
39             ){
40             }
41     return(pjob);
42     }
43
44 int isch_hndlr(ptn) ITRN ptn;{
45     int err = FALSE;
46     switch(ptn->code){
47     case ISCH_REQJOB:
48             err = isch_reqjob(ptn);
49             break;
50     case ITC_ACKOP:
51             err = isch_ackop(ptn);
52             break;
53             }
54     free(ptn);
55     return(err);
56     }
57
58 #define NBOPS (rand()%5 + 10)
59
60 int isch_reqjob(preq) itrn_reqjob_t * preq;{
61     int err = FALSE;
62     int nbops = NBOPS;
```

```
63      job_t * pjob;
64      int opid;
65      bop_t * pbop;
66      /* CREATE A JOB, WITH BATCH OPERATIONS */
67      pjob = (job_t *)MALLOC(sizeof(job_t));
68      pjob->jobid = preq->jobid;
69      pjob->current_op = 0;
70      pjob->boplist = ILST_CREATE;
71      for (opid=0; opid<nbops; opid++){
72              pbop = (bop_t*)MALLOC(sizeof(bop_t));
73              pbop->complete = pbop->triggered = FALSE;
74              ILST_APPEND(pjob->boplist,pbop);
75              }
76      ILST_APPEND(joblist,pjob);
77      /* PERFORM SCHEDULE EXECUTION */
78      isch_process();
79      return(err);
80      }
81
82  int isch_ackop(ptn) itrn_ackop_t * ptn;{
83      int err = FALSE;
84      job_t * pjob;
85      bop_t * pbop;
86      /* MARK COMPLETION OF CURRENT BATCH OPERATION */
87      pjob = isch_findjob(ptn->jobid);
88      if (pjob==NULL){
89              /* ERROR */
90              }
91      if (ptn->opid != pjob->current_op){
92              /* ERROR */
93              }
94      pbop = ILST_NTH(pjob->boplist,pjob->current_op);
95      if (!pbop){
96              /* ERROR */
97              }
98      pbop->complete = TRUE;
99      /* PERFORM SCHEDULE EXECUTION */
100     isch_process();
101     return(err);
102     }
103
104 ILST isch_free_boplist(list) ILST list;{
105     ILST l;
106     while(list!=NULL){
107             l = list->next;
108             free(list->thing);
109             free(list);
110             list = l;
111             }
112     return(NULL);
113     }
114
115 isch_process(){
116     job_t * pjob;
117     bop_t * pbop;
118     /* FOR EACH JOB */
119     for (pjob=ILST_FIRST(joblist);
120             pjob!=NULL;
```

```
121              pjob=ILST_NEXT(joblist,pjob)
122              ){
123              /* IF CURRENT OP COMPLETE, INCREMENT TO NEXT OP */
124              pbop = ILST_NTH(pjob->boplist,pjob->current_op);
125              if (pbop && pbop->complete){
126                      pjob->current_op++;
127              }
128              /* IF JOB IS DONE */
129              pbop = ILST_NTH(pjob->boplist,pjob->current_op);
130              if (pbop==NULL){
131                      /* SEND ACKJOB TRANSACTION */
132                      itrn_ackjob_t * ptrn;
133                      ptrn = (itrn_ackjob_t*)MALLOC(sizeof(itrn_ackjob_t));
134                      ptrn->code = ISCH_ACKJOB;
135                      ptrn->jobid = pjob->jobid;
136                      /* DELETE JOB */
137                      isch_free_boplist(pjob->boplist);
138                      ILST_DELETE(joblist,pjob);
139                      itrn_put(ptrn);
140                      /* DON'T CHECK FOR TRIGGERING */
141                      free(pjob);
142                      continue;
143              }
144              /* IF CURRENT OP NOT YET TRIGGERED */
145              if (!pbop->triggered){
146                      /* TRIGGER CURRENT OPERATION */
147                      itrn_reqop_t * ptrn;
148                      pbop->triggered = TRUE;
149                      /* SEND OPERATION REQUEST TO TASK COORDINATOR */
150                      ptrn = (itrn_reqop_t*)MALLOC(sizeof(itrn_reqop_t));
151                      ptrn->code = ITC_REQOP;
152                      ptrn->jobid = pjob->jobid;
153                      ptrn->opid = pjob->current_op;
154                      itrn_put(ptrn);
155              }
156      }
157 }
```

It has a single main handler *isch_hndlr* that branches off to two subordinate handlers, *isch_reqjob* and *isch_ackop*. When a job is requested, the job structure is created along with a list of batch operations. Then *isch_process* is called, which decides what to do next. Handler *isch_ackop* receives operation-complete acknowledgements. It records the new status information and calls *isch_process* to take further action. *isch_process* is the brains of the module. It looks for operations that have just completed and either requests the next operation or acknowledges completion of the job.

The following file *itc.c* contains the task coordinator module. It receives requests for batch operations and sequences, each one through its individual device control and material handling tasks:

```
1 /* itc.c task coordinator transaction handler */
2
3 #include <stdio.h>
```

```
 4 #include "ignl.h"
 5 #include "ilst.h"
 6 #include "itrn.h"
 7 #include "itrndef.h"
 8
 9 #if 0
10 On completion of mh move or device operation complete
11     determine next task to do and request it
12     If no next task in operation,
13             signal operation complete to schedule execution
14             record operation complete in database
15
16 On start-operation request from schedule execution,
17     determine next task to do and trigger it
18     record operation-started in database
19
20 #endif
21
22 /* THERE IS A LIST OF OPERATIONS, EACH WITH A LIST OF TASKS */
23
24 ILST oplist;
25 int next_op;
26
27 typedef struct operation_struct {
28     int id;
29     int current_task;
30     ILST tasklist;
31     int jobid;
32     } operation_t;
33
34 ILST itc_free_tasks(list) ILST list;{
35     ILST l;
36     while(list!=NULL){
37             l = list->next;
38             free(list->thing);
39             free(list);
40             list = l;
41             }
42     return(NULL);
43     }
44
45 typedef struct task_struct {
46     int id;
47     int type;
48     int triggered, complete;
49     } task_t;
50
51 int itc_hndlr(ptn) ITRN ptn;{
52     int err = FALSE;
53     switch(ptn->code){
54     case ITC_REQOP:
55             err = itc_reqop(ptn);
56             break;
57     case IMH_ACKMOVE:
58             err = itc_ack_mh(ptn);
59             break;
60     case IDEV_ACKTSK:
61             err = itc_ack_idev(ptn);
```

```
 62                 break;
 63                 }
 64        free(ptn);
 65        return(err);
 66        }
 67
 68   #define NTASKS 10
 69
 70   /* HANDLE START-OPERATION REQUEST */
 71   int itc_reqop(preq) itrn_reqop_t * preq;{
 72        int err = FALSE;
 73        int i;
 74        operation_t * ptop;
 75        task_t * ptask;
 76        /* CREATE OPERATION REQUEST */
 77        ptop = (operation_t *)MALLOC(sizeof(operation_t));
 78        ptop->id = next_op++;
 79        ptop->tasklist = ILST_CREATE;
 80        ptop->current_task = 0;
 81        ptop->jobid = preq->jobid;
 82        for (i=0; i<NTASKS; i++){
 83                ptask = (task_t *)MALLOC(sizeof(task_t));
 84                ptask->id = i;
 85                ptask->type = i % 2;
 86                ptask->triggered = FALSE;
 87                ptask->complete = FALSE;
 88                ILST_APPEND(ptop->tasklist,ptask);
 89                }
 90        ILST_APPEND(oplist,ptop);
 91        /* DO TASK COORDINATOR PROCESSING */
 92        err = itc_process();
 93        return(err);
 94        }
 95
 96   int itc_ack_mh(ptn) itrn_ackmh_t * ptn;{
 97        int err = FALSE;
 98        operation_t * ptop;
 99        task_t * ptask;
100        /* FIND RELEVANT OPERATION REQUEST */
101        for (   ptop = ILST_FIRST(oplist);
102                ptop != NULL;
103                ptop = ILST_NEXT(oplist,ptop)
104                ){
105                if (ptop->id==ptn->mvid) break;
106                }
107        if (ptop==NULL){
108                /* ERROR: INVALID OPERATION ID */
109                }
110        /* THE CURRENT TASK SHOULD BE AN MH MOVE */
111        ptask = ILST_NTH(ptop->tasklist,ptop->current_task);
112        if (ptask->type != 0){
113                /* ERROR: TASK TYPE MISMATCH */
114                }
115        /* MARK THE TASK COMPLETE AND ADVANCE TO NEXT */
116        ptask->complete = TRUE;
117        ptop->current_task ++;
118        /* DO TASK COORDINATOR PROCESSING */
119        err = itc_process();
```

```
120     return(err);
121     }
122
123 int itc_ack_idev(ptn) itrn_acktsk_t * ptn;{
124     int err = FALSE;
125     operation_t * ptop;
126     task_t * ptask;
127     /* FIND RELEVANT OPERATION REQUEST */
128     for (   ptop = ILST_FIRST(oplist);
129             ptop != NULL;
130             ptop = ILST_NEXT(oplist,ptop)
131             ){
132             if (ptop->id==ptn->tskid) break;
133             }
134     if (ptop==NULL){
135             /* ERROR: INVALID OPERATION ID */
136             }
137     /* THE CURRENT TASK SHOULD BE A DEVICE OPERATION */
138     ptask = ILST_NTH(ptop->tasklist,ptop->current_task);
139     if (ptask->type != 1){
140             /* ERROR: TASK TYPE MISMATCH */
141             }
142     /* MARK THE TASK COMPLETE AND ADVANCE TO NEXT */
143     ptask->complete = TRUE;
144     ptop->current_task ++;
145     /* DO TASK COORDINATOR PROCESSING */
146     err = itc_process();
147     return(err);
148     }
149
150 int itc_process(){
151     int err = FALSE;
152     operation_t * ptop;
153     task_t * ptask;
154     /* FOR EACH OPERATION REQUEST */
155     for (   ptop = ILST_FIRST(oplist);
156             ptop != NULL;
157             ptop = ILST_NEXT(oplist,ptop)
158             ){
159             /* IF ALL TASKS DONE, SEND ITC_ACKOP AND DELETE OP */
160             if (ptop->current_task >= ILST_LENGTH(ptop->tasklist)){
161                     itrn_ackop_t * p_ack;
162                     p_ack = (itrn_ackop_t *)MALLOC(sizeof(itrn_ackop_t));
163                     p_ack->code = ITC_ACKOP;
164                     p_ack->jobid = ptop->jobid;
165                     p_ack->opid = ptop->id;
166                     itrn_put(p_ack);
167                     ptop->tasklist = itc_free_tasks(ptop->tasklist);
168                     ILST_DELETE(oplist,ptop);
169                     free(ptop);
170                     }
171             /* IF NEXT TASK CAN BE TRIGGERED, DO SO */
172             else {
173                     ptask = ILST_NTH(ptop->tasklist,ptop->current_task);
174                     if (!ptask->triggered){
175                             if (ptask->type==0){
176                                     itrn_reqmh_t * p_req;
177                                     p_req = (itrn_reqmh_t *)
                                            MALLOC(sizeof(itrn_reqmh_t));
```

```
178                                   p_req->code = IMH_REQMOVE;
179                                   p_req->mvid = ptop->id;
180                                   itrn_put(p_req);
181                               }
182                           else if (ptask->type==1){
183                                   itrn_reqtsk_t * p_req;
184                                   p_req = (itrn_reqtsk_t *)
                                       MALLOC(sizeof(itrn_reqtsk_t));
185                                   p_req->code = IDEV_REQTSK;
186                                   p_req->tskid = ptop->id;
187                                   itrn_put(p_req);
188                               }
189                           ptask->triggered = TRUE;
190                       }
191                   }
192           }
193       return(err);
194       }
```

It works very much like *isch*. The transactions it receives are requests for operations and acknowledgements of tasks. It keeps a list of operations underway, and a list of tasks for each operation. After each transaction is dealt with, it calls *itc_process* to decide what to do next. Typically, the next thing to do is request another task of device control or material handling.

The following two files contain the simulation for material handling *imh.c* and device control *idev.c*. Since these are just no-ops, on receiving a request transaction, all they do is turn around and send an acknowledgment.

```
 1 /* imh.c material handling transaction handler */
 2
 3 #include <stdio.h>
 4 #include "ignl.h"
 5 #include "ilst.h"
 6 #include "itrn.h"
 7 #include "itrndef.h"
 8 #include "imh.h"
 9
10 #if 0
11 On request for mh move
12     queue up the request.
13     If a cart can initiate the move, initiate it.
14
15 On cart transit completion
16     If this is the completion of a mh move request,
17             send completion request to requester.
18     See which move request should be handled next,
19             and initiate the card transit.
20
21 #endif
22
23 int imh_hndlr(ptn) ITRN ptn;{
24     int err = FALSE;
25     switch(ptn->code){
26     case IMH_REQMOVE:
```

```
27              err = imh_reqmv(ptn);
28              break;
29              }
30      return(err);
31      }
32
33 int imh_reqmv(ptn) ITRN ptn;{
34      int err = FALSE;
35      ptn->code = IMH_ACKMOVE;
36      itrn_put(ptn);
37      return(err);
38      }
```

```
 1 /* idev.c device controller transaction handler */
 2
 3 #include <stdio.h>
 4 #include "ignl.h"
 5 #include "ilst.h"
 6 #include "itrn.h"
 7 #include "itrndef.h"
 8 #include "idev.h"
 9
10 #if 0
11 On request for processing on a device
12     queue up the request
13     If the device can handle the request now, initiate it.
14
15 On completion of processing on a device
16     signal operation completion to the requester.
17     if any further request for the device can be served,
18              initiate it.
19
20 #endif
21
22 int idev_hndlr(ptn) ITRN ptn;{
23      int err = FALSE;
24      switch(ptn->code){
25      case IDEV_REQTSK:
26              err = idev_reqtsk(ptn);
27              break;
28              }
29      return(err);
30      }
31
32 int idev_reqtsk(ptn) ITRN ptn;{
33      int err = FALSE;
34      ptn->code = IDEV_ACKTSK;
35      itrn_put(ptn);
36      return(err);
37      }
```

File *ilst.c* contains the implementation of the list cluster routines, and file *itrn.c* contains the transaction cluster routines.

```
 1 /* ilst.c  list cluster primitives */
 2
 3 #include <stdio.h>
 4 #include "ignl.h"
 5 #include "ilst.h"
 6
 7 ILST ilst_append(list,thing) ILST list; void * thing;{
 8     ILST l = list;
 9     if (list==NULL){
10             list = (ILST)MALLOC(sizeof(*list));
11             list->next = NULL;
12             list->thing = thing;
13             return(list);
14             }
15     for (l=list; l->next != NULL; l = l->next);
16     l->next = (ILST)MALLOC(sizeof(*list));
17     l->next->next = NULL;
18     l->next->thing = thing;
19     return(list);
20     }
21
22 void * ilst_next(list,thing) ILST list; void * thing;{
23     for (; list != NULL && list->thing != thing; list = list->next);
24     if (list==NULL) return(NULL);
25     else if (list->next==NULL) return(NULL);
26     else return(list->next->thing);
27     }
28
29 void * ilst_nth(list,n) ILST list; int n;{
30     for (; list!=NULL && n>0; list=list->next, --n);
31     if (list==NULL) return(NULL);
32     else return(list->thing);
33     }
34
35 int ilst_length(list) ILST list;{
36     int n;
37     for (n=0; list!=NULL; list=list->next, ++n);
38     return(n);
39     }
40
41 ILST ilst_delete(list,thing) ILST list; void * thing;{
42     ILST l;
43     if (list==NULL) return(list);
44     if (list->thing==thing){
45             l = list->next;
46             free(list);
47             return(l);
48             }
49     if (list->next==NULL) return(list);
50     for (l=list; l->next!=NULL && l->next->thing!=thing; l=l->next);
51     if (l->next!=NULL){
52             ILST next = l->next->next;
53             free(l->next);
54             l->next = next;
55             }
56     return(list);
57     }
```

```
 1  /* itrn.c */
 2
 3  #include "itrn.h"
 4  #include "ilst.h"
 5
 6  ILST trnque;
 7
 8  void itrn_put(ptrn) ITRN ptrn;{
 9      ILST_APPEND(trnque,ptrn);
10      }
11
12  ITRN itrn_examine(){
13      return(ILST_FIRST(trnque));
14      }
15
16  ITRN itrn_get(){
17      ITRN ptrn;
18      ptrn = ILST_FIRST(trnque);
19      ILST_DELETE(trnque,ptrn);
20      return(ptrn);
21      }
```

Appendix C. CIM Simulation—Redesign

The header file *fast.h* defines dispatching macros *DISPATCHn*:

```
 1 #define DISPATCH0
 2
 3 #define DISPATCH1 \
 4     if (p->state==1) goto L1;\
 5     DISPATCH0
 6
 7 #define DISPATCH2 \
 8     if (p->state==2) goto L2;\
 9     DISPATCH1
10
11 #define DISPATCH3 \
12     if (p->state==3) goto L3;\
13     DISPATCH2
14
15 #define DISPATCH4 \
16     if (p->state==4) goto L4;\
17     DISPATCH3
18
```

The simulation program is contained in *fast.c*:

```
 1 /* fast.c */
 2
 3 #include <stdio.h>
 4 #include "fast.h"
```

```
 5
 6  #define STDVARS int (*func)(); int state; struct machine_struct *caller
 7
 8  typedef struct machine_struct {
 9      STDVARS;
10      } machine_t;
11
12  #define PROLOGUE(typ,f)\
13      typ *p = (typ*)malloc(sizeof(*p));\
14      extern int f();\
15      p->caller = caller;\
16      p->func = f;\
17      p->state = 0;\
18      (*p->func)(p);
19
20  #define BREAK(n,lab) p->state=(n); enque(p); return; lab:
21
22  #define CALL(n,lab,expr) p->state=(n); (expr); return; lab:
23
24  machine_t * ptemp=NULL;
25
26  int retn_val=0;
27
28  #define RETURN(v)\
29      ptemp=p->caller;\
30      retn_val=(v);\
31      free(p);\
32      if (ptemp){(*ptemp->func)(ptemp);};
33
34  int enq=0, deq=0, ninq=0;
35  machine_t *queue[256];
36  enque(p) machine_t *p;{
37      queue[enq++] = p;
38      if (enq>=256) enq=0;
39      ninq++;
40      }
41
42  machine_t * deque(){
43      machine_t *p = NULL;
44      if (ninq){
45              p = queue[deq++];
46              if (deq>=256) deq=0;
47              ninq--;
48              }
49      return(p);
50      }
51
52  int jobs_started=0;
53  int jobs_completed=0;
54  #define NBOPS (rand()%5 + 10)
55  #define NTASK 10
56  #define NJOBS 100
57
58  main(){
59      machine_t *p;
60      /* REPEAT UNTIL ALL JOBS ARE COMPLETE */
61      while(jobs_completed < NJOBS){
62              /* RUN WHATEVER CAN BE RUN */
```

```
63                 if (ninq){
64                     p = deque();
65                     (*p->func)(p);
66                     }
67             /* IF < 100 JOBS STARTED AND < 10 JOBS IN PROCESS */
68             if (jobs_started<NJOBS && jobs_started-jobs_completed < 10){
69                 /* START ANOTHER JOB */
70                 job(NULL);
71                 }
72         }
73     }
74
75 typedef struct {
76     STDVARS;
77     int jobid;
78     int i;
79     int nbops;
80     } job_t;
81 job(caller) machine_t *caller;{
82     PROLOGUE(job_t,job_func);
83     }
84 job_func(p) job_t *p;{
85     DISPATCH1;
86     p->jobid = jobs_started++;
87     p->nbops = NBOPS;
88     /* FOR EACH OPERATION */
89     for (p->i=0; p->i < p->nbops; p->i++){
90             CALL(1,L1,opn(p));
91             }
92     jobs_completed++;
93     printf("Ack Job %d\n",p->jobid);
94     RETURN(1);
95     }
96
97 typedef struct {
98     STDVARS;
99     int taskid;
100    int ntask;
101    } opn_t;
102 opn(caller) machine_t *caller;{
103    PROLOGUE(opn_t,opn_func);
104    }
105 opn_func(p) opn_t *p;{
106    DISPATCH2;
107    p->ntask = NTASK;
108    /* FOR EACH OPERATION */
109    for (p->taskid=0; p->taskid < p->ntask; p->taskid++){
110            CALL(1,L1,dev_ctl(p));
111            CALL(2,L2,mh_ctl(p));
112            }
113    RETURN(1);
114    }
115
116 typedef struct {
117    STDVARS;
118    } dev_ctl_t;
119 dev_ctl(caller) machine_t *caller;{
120    PROLOGUE(dev_ctl_t,dev_ctl_func);
```

```
121        }
122 dev_ctl_func(p) dev_ctl_t *p;{
123        DISPATCH1;
124        /* DO SOMETHING */
125        BREAK(1,L1);
126        RETURN(1);
127        }
128
129 typedef struct {
130        STDVARS;
131        } mh_ctl_t;
132 mh_ctl(caller) machine_t *caller;{
133        PROLOGUE(mh_ctl_t,mh_ctl_func);
134        }
135 mh_ctl_func(p) mh_ctl_t *p;{
136        DISPATCH1;
137        /* DO SOMETHING */
138        BREAK(1,L1);
139        RETURN(1);
140        }
141
142
```

The definition of the little language occupies lines 6–50.

The *main* routine (line 58) simply runs the dispatching loop until everything is done, starting new jobs when appropriate.

The *job* state machine is in lines 75–95. It consists of a record, a procedure to start a job, and the main function. The main function simply assigns a job ID and performs as many operations as necessary in a loop. As an *operation* is another state machine, the *CALL* macro is used, which waits for the subordinate state machine to complete.

The operation state machine *opn* is defined similarly, in lines 97–114.

The device-control and material-handling state machines occupy lines 115–140. Each is a no-op except that it does a *BREAK* to give up control so that other processes can run in parallel with it. In real life this corresponds to waiting for asynchronous input from external hardware.

Appendix D. Two-Phase DIFEX

```
 1 /* fm.h Copyright Michael R. Dunlavey 1987 */
 2
 3 #define GMODE_ERASE 1
 4 #define GMODE_SHOW 2
 5 #define GMODE_UPDATE 3
 6
 7 #ifdef IN_FM
 8 #define DEF_VAR(typ, name, init) typ name = init
 9 #define DEF_ARRAY(typ, name, size) typ name[size]
10 #else
11 #define DEF_VAR(typ, name, init) extern typ name
12 #define DEF_ARRAY(typ, name, size) extern typ name[]
13 #endif
14
15
16 DEF_VAR(char, fm_mode, GMODE_SHOW);
17 DEF_VAR(char, fm_phase, 0);
18 DEF_VAR(char far *, fm_buffer, NULL);
19 DEF_VAR(char far *, fm_pold, NULL);
20 DEF_VAR(char far *, fm_pnew, NULL);
21 DEF_ARRAY(char, fm_newspace, 1<<14);
22
23 #define NEW_LEN (fm_pnew - (char far *)fm_newspace)
24
25 #define GETINT(var) ((var) = *((int*)fm_pold)++)
26 #define PUTINT(var) (*((int*)fm_pnew)++ = (var))
27
28 #define GETLONG(var) ((var) = *((long*)fm_pold)++)
29 #define PUTLONG(var) (*((long*)fm_pnew)++ = (var))
30
31 #define MASKOF_INT (sizeof(int)-1)
32
33 #define GETSTR(var){\
```

```
34        char far * fm_v=(var);\
35        while(*fm_v++ = *fm_pold++);\
36        if ((long)fm_pold & 1) fm_pold++;\
37        }
38
39 #define PUTSTR(var){\
40        char far * fm_v=(var);\
41        while(*fm_pnew++ = *fm_v++);\
42                if ((long)fm_pnew & 1) *fm_pnew++ = 0;\
43        }
44
45 #define PROTECT(expr) (fm_mode==GMODE_ERASE ? 0 : (expr))
46
47 #define IF(test) {char save_mode = fm_mode;\
48      if (if_util((int)PROTECT(test))){
49
50 #define FOR(init,test,step) {char save_mode = fm_mode;\
51      for(PROTECT(init); if_util((int)PROTECT(test)); PROTECT(step)){
52
53 #define SWITCH(v){\
54      int save_mode = fm_mode;\
55      int val_array[4],mode_array[2],switch_index;\
56      fm_swutil((v),val_array,mode_array);\
57      for (fm_mode = mode_array[0]; fm_mode <= mode_array[1]; fm_mode++)\
58              switch(val_array[fm_mode]){
59
60
61 #define END } fm_mode = save_mode;}
62
63 #define fm_gpfarptr(a,b) fm_gplong((a),(b))
64
65 extern void fm_init(/* f */) /* void (*f)() */ ;
66
67 extern void fm_view();
68
69 extern void fm_erase();
70
71
```

```
1 /* fm.c Copyright Michael R. Dunlavey 1987 */
2
3 #include <stdio.h>
4 #include <malloc.h>
5
6 #define IN_FM
7 #include "fm.h"
8
9 void fm_gpint(vget,vput) int *vget,*vput;{
10     switch (fm_mode){
11             case GMODE_SHOW:
12                     if (fm_phase == 1)
13                             PUTINT(*vput);
14                     break;
15             case GMODE_ERASE:
16                     GETINT(*vget);
```

```
17                      if (fm_phase == 0)
18                              PUTINT(*vget);
19                      break;
20              case GMODE_UPDATE:
21                      GETINT(*vget);
22                      if (fm_phase == 0)
23                              PUTINT(*vget);
24                      else
25                              PUTINT(*vput);
26                      break;
27              }
28      }
29
30 void fm_gplong(vget,vput) long *vget,*vput;{
31      switch (fm_mode){
32              case GMODE_SHOW:
33                      if (fm_phase == 1)
34                              PUTLONG(*vput);
35                      break;
36              case GMODE_ERASE:
37                      GETLONG(*vget);
38                      if (fm_phase == 0)
39                              PUTLONG(*vget);
40                      break;
41              case GMODE_UPDATE:
42                      GETLONG(*vget);
43                      if (fm_phase == 0)
44                              PUTLONG(*vget);
45                      else
46                              PUTLONG(*vput);
47                      break;
48              }
49      }
50
51 void fm_gpstr(sget,sput) char *sget,*sput;{
52      switch (fm_mode){
53              case GMODE_SHOW:
54                      if (fm_phase == 1)
55                              PUTSTR(sput)
56                      break;
57              case GMODE_ERASE:
58                      GETSTR(sget);
59                      if (fm_phase == 0)
60                              PUTSTR(sget)
61                      break;
62              case GMODE_UPDATE:
63                      GETSTR(sget);
64                      if (fm_phase == 0)
65                              PUTSTR(sget)
66                      else
67                              PUTSTR(sput);
68                      break;
69              }
70      }
71
72 int if_util(test) int test;{
73      int old_test,retn_value = 1;
74      if (test) test = 1;
```

```
75      fm_gpint(&old_test,&test);
76      switch(fm_mode){
77      case GMODE_ERASE:
78              retn_value = old_test;
79              break;
80      case GMODE_SHOW:
81              retn_value = test;
82              break;
83      case GMODE_UPDATE:
84              if (test == old_test)
85                      retn_value = test;
86              else if (test)
87                      fm_mode = GMODE_SHOW;
88              else
89                      fm_mode = GMODE_ERASE;
90              break;
91              }
92      return(retn_value);
93      }
94
95  int fm_swutil(val,va,ma) int va[],ma[];{
96      int old_val;
97      fm_gpint(&old_val,&val);
98      ma[0] = ma[1] = fm_mode;
99      switch(fm_mode){
100     case GMODE_ERASE:
101             va[GMODE_ERASE] = old_val;
102             break;
103     case GMODE_SHOW:
104             va[GMODE_SHOW] = val;
105             break;
106     case GMODE_UPDATE:
107             if (val != old_val){
108                     ma[0] = GMODE_ERASE; va[GMODE_ERASE] = old_val;
109                     ma[1] = GMODE_SHOW; va[GMODE_SHOW] = val;
110                     }
111             else {
112                     va[GMODE_UPDATE] = val;
113                     }
114             break;
115             }
116     }
117
118 unsigned int fm_buflen = 0;
119
120 static void (*fm_display)();
121
122 void fm_init(f) void (*f)(); {
123     fm_display = f;
124     /* FREE OLD BUFFER AND ALLOCATE NEW */
125     if (fm_buffer)
126             _ffree(fm_buffer);
127     fm_buffer = NULL;
128     fm_buflen = 0;
129     fm_pold = NULL;
130     fm_pnew = fm_newspace;
131     fm_mode = GMODE_SHOW;
132     }
```

```
133
134 int fm_end_pass(){
135     register int n;
136     register char far * pnew;
137     register char far * pbuf;
138     /* IF WE NEED A BIGGER BUFFER, FREE THE OLD ONE */
139     if (NEW_LEN > fm_buflen){
140             if (fm_buffer) _ffree(fm_buffer); /**/
141             fm_buffer = NULL;
142             fm_buflen = 0;
143             }
144     /* IF WE NEED A NEW BUFFER, ALLOCATE IT */
145     if (!fm_buffer){
146             fm_buflen = NEW_LEN;
147             fm_buffer = (char far *)_fmalloc( fm_buflen * sizeof(int) );
148             }
149     /* IF COULDN'T ALLOCATE IT, EXIT */
150     if (!fm_buffer){
151             exit(0);
152             }
153     /* COPY NEW DATA INTO BUFFER */
154     pbuf = fm_buffer;
155     pnew = fm_newspace;
156     n = NEW_LEN;
157     while(1){
158             if (n >= 4){
159                     *pbuf++ = *pnew++;
160                     *pbuf++ = *pnew++;
161                     *pbuf++ = *pnew++;
162                     *pbuf++ = *pnew++;
163                     n -= 4;
164                     }
165             else if (n > 0){
166                     *pbuf++ = *pnew++;
167                     n--;
168                     }
169             else break;
170             }
171     /* RESET NEW POINTER TO START OF NEWSPACE */
172     fm_pnew = fm_newspace;
173     /* RESET OLD POINTER TO START OF BUFFER */
174     fm_pold = fm_buffer;
175     /* NOW READY FOR NEXT PASS */
176     }
177
178 void fm_view(){
179     for (fm_phase=0; fm_phase < 2; fm_phase++){
180             (*fm_display)();
181             fm_end_pass();
182             }
183     if (fm_mode==GMODE_SHOW)
184             fm_mode = GMODE_UPDATE;
185     }
186
187 void fm_erase(){
188     fm_mode = GMODE_ERASE;
189     for (fm_phase=0; fm_phase < 2; fm_phase++){
190             (*fm_display)();
```

```
191               fm_end_pass();
192           }
193     }
194
195
```

```
 1 /* rtest.c  test of two-phase differential execution */
 2 #include <stdio.h>
 3 #include <malloc.h>
 4 #include <graph.h>  /* MS graphics library */
 5 #include "fm.h"
 6
 7 struct box_struct { /* bounding box structure */
 8     int x0,x1,y0,y1;
 9     int mark,color;
10     };
11
12 int passnum = 0;
13 int nbox = 0;                   /* number of boxes */
14 struct box_struct far * boxtab[2000];        /* bounding box table */
15
16 #define SWAP(a,b){register int temp=(a);(a)=(b);(b)=temp;}
17
18 /* mark all boxes that overlap this one */
19 mark_overlap(x0,y0,x1,y1,mark,color){
20     int i;
21     if (x1<x0) SWAP(x1,x0);
22     if (y1<y0) SWAP(y1,y0);
23     for (i=0; i<nbox; i++){
24             register struct box_struct far * p = boxtab[i];
25             if (x0 <= p->x1 && x1 >= p->x0 && y0 <= p->y1 && y1 >= p->y0){
26                     p->mark = mark;
27                     p->color = color;
28                     }
29             }
30     }
31
32 /* initialize a box */
33 set_box(p,x0,y0,x1,y1,mark,color) struct box_struct far * p;{
34     if (x1<x0) SWAP(x1,x0);
35     if (y1<y0) SWAP(y1,y0);
36     p->x0 = x0; p->x1 = x1;
37     p->y0 = y0; p->y1 = y1;
38     p->mark = mark;
39     p->color = color;
40     }
41
42 /* add a new bos to box table  */
43 struct box_struct far * add_box(x0,y0,x1,y1,mark,color){
44     register struct box_struct far * p;
45     p = (struct box_struct far *)_fmalloc(sizeof(struct box_struct));
46     boxtab[nbox++] = p;
47     set_box(p,x0,y0,x1,y1,mark,color);
48     return(p);
49     }
```

```
50
51  /* remove a box from box table */
52  del_box(struct box_struct far * p){
53      int i;
54      for (i=0; i<nbox; i++) if (p==boxtab[i]) break;
55      for (i++; i<nbox; i++) boxtab[i-1] = boxtab[i];
56      nbox--;
57      }
58
59  /* maintain a line on the screen */
60  draw_a_line(x0,y0,x1,y1,color){
61      int old_x0,old_y0,old_x1,old_y1,old_color;
62      int redraw;
63      struct box_struct far * p;
64      fm_gpint(&old_x0,&x0);
65      fm_gpint(&old_y0,&y0);
66      fm_gpint(&old_x1,&x1);
67      fm_gpint(&old_y1,&y1);
68      fm_gpint(&old_color,&color);
69      if (fm_mode==GMODE_SHOW && fm_phase == 1){
70              p = add_box(x0,y0,x1,y1,passnum,color);
71              }
72      fm_gpfarptr(&p,&p);
73      switch(fm_mode){
74      case GMODE_SHOW:
75              if (fm_phase == 1){
76                      /* DRAW THE LINE */
77                      _setcolor(color);
78                      _moveto(x0,y0);
79                      _lineto(x1,y1);
80                      mark_overlap(x0,y0,x1,y1,passnum,color);
81                      }
82              break;
83      case GMODE_ERASE:
84              if (fm_phase==0){
85                      del_box(p);
86                      /* ERASE THE LINE */
87                      _setcolor(0);
88                      _moveto(old_x0,old_y0);
89                      _lineto(old_x1,old_y1);
90                      mark_overlap(old_x0,old_y0,old_x1,old_y1,passnum,0);
91                      _ffree(p);
92                      }
93              break;
94      case GMODE_UPDATE:
95              redraw = (
96                      x0!=old_x0
97                      || y0!=old_y0
98                      || x1!=old_x1
99                      || y1!=old_y1
100                     || color!=old_color
101                     || p->mark==passnum
102                     );
103             if (fm_phase==0){
104                     if (redraw){
105                             /* ERASE THE LINE */
106                             _setcolor(0);
107                             _moveto(old_x0,old_y0);
```

```
108                             _lineto(old_x1,old_y1);
109                             mark_overlap(old_x0,old_y0,old_x1,old_y1
110                                 ,passnum,0);
111                         }
112                     }
113             if (fm_phase==1){
114                     if (redraw){
115                             /* DRAW THE LINE */
116                             _setcolor(color);
117                             _moveto(x0,y0);
118                             _lineto(x1,y1);
119                             mark_overlap(x0,y0,x1,y1,passnum,color);
120                             set_box(p,x0,y0,x1,y1,passnum,color);
121                     }
122             }
123         break;
124         }
125     }
126
127 /* maintain a solid rectangle on the screen */
128 draw_a_rect(x0,y0,x1,y1,color){
129     int old_x0,old_y0,old_x1,old_y1,old_color;
130     int redraw;
131     struct box_struct far * p;
132     fm_gpint(&old_x0,&x0);
133     fm_gpint(&old_y0,&y0);
134     fm_gpint(&old_x1,&x1);
135     fm_gpint(&old_y1,&y1);
136     fm_gpint(&old_color,&color);
137     if (fm_mode==GMODE_SHOW && fm_phase == 1){
138             p = add_box(x0,y0,x1,y1,passnum,color);
139             }
140     fm_gpfarptr(&p,&p);
141     switch(fm_mode){
142     case GMODE_SHOW:
143             if (fm_phase==1){
144                     /* DRAW THE RECTANGLE */
145                     _setcolor(color);
146                     _rectangle(_GFILLINTERIOR,x0,y0,x1,y1);
147                     mark_overlap(x0,y0,x1,y1,passnum,color);
148                     }
149             break;
150     case GMODE_UPDATE:
151             redraw = (
152                     x0!=old_x0
153                     || y0!=old_y0
154                     || x1!=old_x1
155                     || y1!=old_y1
156                     || color!=old_color
157                     || p->mark==passnum
158                     );
159             if (fm_phase==0){
160                     if (redraw){
161                             /* ERASE THE RECTANGLE */
162                             _setcolor(0);
163                             _rectangle(_GFILLINTERIOR
164                                 ,old_x0,old_y0,old_x1,old_y1
165                                 );
```

```
166                                    mark_overlap(old_x0,old_y0,old_x1,old_y1
167                                          ,passnum,0
168                                          );
169                                    }
170                              }
171                  if (fm_phase==1){
172                        if (redraw){
173                              /* DRAW THE RECTANGLE */
174                              _setcolor(color);
175                              _rectangle(_GFILLINTERIOR,x0,y0,x1,y1);
176                              mark_overlap(x0,y0,x1,y1,passnum,color);
177                              set_box(p,x0,y0,x1,y1,passnum,color);
178                              }
179                        }
180            break;
181      case GMODE_ERASE:
182            if (fm_phase==0){
183                  del_box(p);
184                  /* ERASE THE RECTANGLE */
185                  _setcolor(0);
186                  _rectangle(_GFILLINTERIOR
187                        ,old_x0,old_y0,old_x1,old_y1
188                        );
189                  mark_overlap(old_x0,old_y0,old_x1,old_y1
190                        ,passnum,0
191                        );
192                  _ffree(p);
193                  }
194            break;
195            }
196      }
197
198 /* ----------------------------------------------------------------- */
199 /*     "Application" code.        */
200
201 int xo = 300, yo = 100;
202
203 int b = 0;
204 int x = 10;
205 int y = 10;
206 int vx = 8, vy = 10;
207
208 /* display consists of three rectangles
209    plus one that bounces and blinks */
210 display(){
211    draw_a_rect(xo+0,yo+0,xo+40,yo+100,1);
212    IF(b)
213          draw_a_rect(xo+x,yo+y,xo+x+80,yo+y+20,2);
214          END
215    draw_a_rect(xo+120,yo+0,xo+160,yo+100,7);
216    draw_a_rect(xo+60,yo+0,xo+100,yo+100,4);
217    }
218
219 /* main routine */
220 main(){
221    _setvideomode(_ERESCOLOR);          /* setup */
222    _clearscreen(_GCLEARSCREEN);
223    nbox = 0;
```

```
224        passnum = 1;
225        fm_init(display);
226        fm_view();                      /* show */
227        passnum++;
228        getch();
229        b = 1;
230        fm_view(display);               /* update */
231        getch();
232        while(1){                       /* update until 'q' */
233               fm_view();
234               passnum++;
235               if (getch()=='q') break;
236                                         /* bounce logic */
237               if (x <= 0 || x > 80) vx = -vx;
238               if (y <= 0 || y > 80) vy = -vy;
239               x += vx; y += vy;
240               }
241        b = 0;
242        fm_view();                      /* one last update */
243        passnum++;
244        getch();
245        fm_erase();                     /* erase */
246        getch();
247        _setvideomode(_DEFAULTMODE);    /* finish */
248        }
249
250
```

Bibliography

Aho, Ullman. *Principles of Compiler Design*. Reading, MA: Addison-Wesley, 1979.
    The classic text on compiler design.

Attneave, Frederick. *Applications of Information Theory to Psychology*. New York: Holt, Rinehart, and Winston, 1959.
    An excellent and very accessible introduction to the Information Theory of Shannon and Weaver.

Baker, H.G. "List Processing in Real Time on a Serial Computer." In *Communications of the ACM* (April 1978), pp. 280–294.

Bentley, Jon. "Squeezing Constant Factors of Geometric Algorithms." Proceedings of the 19th Allerton Conference, Coordinated Science Laboratory, University of Illinois, Urbana-Champaign, IL, 1981, pp. 11–20.
    In this landmark report, Bentley demonstrates methods for speeding up algorithms by large constant factors. The difference between his approach and ours is that we feel that Information Theory provides a common explanatory structure for what otherwise seems like a random collection of techniques, and therefore points the way toward additional techniques.

———. *Writing Efficient Programs*. Englewood Cliffs, NJ: Prentice-Hall, 1982.

———. *Programming Pearls*. Reading, MA: Addison-Wesley, 1986.

———. *More Programming Pearls*. Reading, MA: Addison-Wesley, 1988.

Boehm, B.W. *Software Engineering Economics*. Englewood Cliffs, NJ: Prentice-Hall, 1981.

———. "A Spiral Model of Software Development and Enhancement." *Computer* (May 1988), pp. 61–72.

Borland International. *Turbo C++ Class Library Definition*. South Valley, CA, 1990.
    A good example of the "class library" concept, or "re-usable code."

Brooks, Fred. "No Silver Bullet: Essence and Accidents of Software Engineering." *Computer* (April 1987), pp. 10–19.

This wonderful short article by the author of *The Mythical Man-Month* debunks many myths and fads, pointing the way toward rapid prototyping and the nurturing of star programmers as key directions in which improvement will be found. We go beyond these ideas by pointing out that those star programmers are not magicians, they are engineers, inventors, artisans. The things they do can be taught to others. We insist that, for the price of a learning curve, there are indeed silver bullets in the form of ideas by which ordinary programmers can create extraordinary software.

Dijkstra, E.W. *A Discipline of Programming*. Englewood Cliffs, NJ: Prentice-Hall, 1976.

Drake, A.W. *Fundamentals of Applied Probability Theory*. New York: McGraw-Hill, 1967.

Dunlavey, Michael. "Query Performance of a Many-Dimensional Best-Match Algorithm." Proceedings of the 19th Allerton Conference on Communication, Control, and Computing, Electrical Engineering Department, University of Illinois at Urbana-Champaign, IL, October 1981, pp. 389–396.

In this technical article I analyze the expected performance of best-match algorithms based on binary tree search. The performance varies smoothly between logarithmic and linear as the distance to the best match increases.

———. "Differential Evaluation: A Method for Incremental Update of Graphical Displays of Structures." *Software Practice and Experience*, Vol. 23, No. 8, London: John Wiley and Sons, 1993, pp. 871–893.

———. "Performance Tuning: Slugging It Out." *Dr. Dobb's Journal*, Vol. 18, No. 12 (November 1993), pp. 18–26.

Furtek, Frederick. *The Logic of Systems*. MIT/LCS/TR-170, Laboratory for Computer Science, Massachusetts Institute of Technology, Cambridge, MA, 1976.

A rigorous approach to defining information in systems represented as Petri nets. He uses a set-theoretic rather than a quantitative approach. It is useful for expanding one's concept of information and its relationship to computer programs.

Guiasu, Silviu. *Information Theory with Applications*. New York: McGraw-Hill, 1977.

A rigorous yet accessible textbook. Its treatment of entropy and coding theory is very good, as well as its discussion of concrete applications.

Halstead, M.H. *Elements of Software Science*. Amsterdam: Elsevier North-Holland, 1977.

Hewitt and Patterson. "Comparative Schematology." Artificial Intelligence Memo No. 201, Massachusetts Institute of Technology, Artificial Intelligence Laboratory, Cambridge, MA, November 1970.

Huffman, D.A. "A Method for the Construction of Minimum-Redundancy Codes." Ed. W. Jackson. *Communication Theory*. London: Butterworths Scientific Publications, 1953.

This technique is also presented in any text on Information Theory (see Guiasu).

Josephson, M. *Edison*. New York: McGraw-Hill Paperbacks, 1959.

Kernighan, B.W., and Ritchie, D.M. *The C Programming Language*. Englewood Cliffs, NJ: Prentice-Hall, 1978.

Minsky, M. *Computation: Finite and Infinite Machines*. Englewood Cliffs, NJ: Prentice-Hall, 1967.

   A very stimulating text, this is very good for learning about finite state machines, pushdown automata, and universal machines. It is also an excellent early perspective on Artificial Intelligence.

Minsky, M., and Papert, S. *Perceptrons*. Cambridge, MA: MIT Press, 1969.

   Contains a clear statement of the best-match problem.

Peterson, J.L. "Computer Programs for Detecting and Correcting Spelling Errors." *Communications of the ACM* (December 1980), pp. 676–687.

Winograd, Terry. "Procedures as a Representation for Data in a Computer Program for Understanding Natural Language." MAC TR-84, Project MAC, Massachusetts Institute of Technology, Cambridge, MA, February 1971. (Also in book form through MIT Press.)

———. *Understanding Natural Language*. New York: Academic Press, 1972.

   This is a landmark thesis in the computer processing of natural language. The complexity of such a problem goes well beyond that of everyday software, and so must the techniques used to solve it. The base language used was Lisp, of course, but beyond that, a key aspect of the design was representing data as procedures in both the syntactic analysis and the knowledge processing.

Winston, P.H. *Artificial Intelligence*. Reading, MA: Addison-Wesley, 1977.

   An excellent teaching and reference text on Artificial Intelligence.

Index